Tales
and Songs
of
Southern
Illinois

Collected by
Charles Neely

Edited with a Foreword
by John Webster Spargo

Southern Illinois University Press
Carbondale and Edwardsville

Copyright © 1938 by Julia Jonah Neely
First edition published 1938 by Julia Jonah Neely and the George Banta
Publishing Company
Reprinted 1989 by Crossfire Press
New edition published 1998 by Southern Illinois University Press,
Carbondale, IL 62902-3697
All rights reserved
Printed in the United States of America
01 00 99 98   4 3 2 1

Library of Congress Cataloging-in-Publication Data
Neely, Charles, 1902–1937.
    Tales and songs of southern Illinois / collected by Charles Neely ;
  edited with a foreword by John Webster Spargo.
        p.   cm.
    Originally published: Menasha, Wis. : George Banta Pub. Co., 1938.
    Includes index.
    1. Tales—Illinois. 2. Folksongs, English—Illinois—Texts.
  I. Spargo, John Webster, 1896–1956. II. Title.
  GR110.I3N43 1998
  398'.09773—dc21   97-34077
                                                                   CIP
    ISBN 0-8093-2183-1 (pbk. : alk. paper)

The paper used in this publication meets the minimum requirements of
American National Standard for Information Sciences—Permanence of
Paper for Printed Library Materials, ANSI Z39.48-1984. ♾

To

JOHN WILLIAM ASHTON

CONTENTS

PART I

FOLK TALES

vii

PART II

BALLADS AND SONGS

FOREWORD

By JOHN WEBSTER SPARGO
Northwestern University

THE TALES and songs in this volume were collected
by Mr. Charles Neely, who was Assistant Professor of English at the Southern Illinois Teachers' College, Carbondale, from 1935 until the time of his
premature death on March 11, 1937. They are the fruits
of Mr. Neely's careful labors for some dozen years or
more in a field hitherto untouched by collectors. They
are of fascinating interest to the folklorist not only because of the blends of cultural influences present but
also because of the way in which Mr. Neely set about
his task of finding them. He gathered in the materials
which came under his observation, not just those which
might have fitted some preconceived definition. Thus
the collection constitutes a cross-section, after a fashion,
of the tales and songs current among the people of
"Egypt" during the past generation and more. Mr.
Neely set up no conditions for admission save that the
tale or song must be *there*, in "Egypt." It was imma-
terial whether the item came to him orally or in writing,
whether it was "Egyptian" or not, whether its ultimate
origin was purely local, the British Isles, the Continent
of Europe, the Wild West of frontier days, the South of
the Civil War, the America of the Red Indian—all was
fish for Mr. Neely's cunningly-laid net. As anyone can
see, the result is an uncommonly varied and interesting
volume of tales and songs.

European folklorists in particular will wish that this
matter of blends could have been worked out more thoroughly than it has been in Mr. Neely's notes. Those who

are collectors will realize the difficulty, nay, the impossibility of securing from the average informant reliable data extending back for a generation or more, especially when the forbears of these informants were on the move, all ultimately from across the sea, many experiencing also several changes, in one generation or another, after arrival in America. These moves, be it noted, whether across ocean, mountain, forest or plain, can hardly be called folk migrations if the latter are regarded as movements of cohesive masses of people. Those European folklorists who are not collectors will agree that the absence of reliable data both as to the make-up of the population of the original settlements and as to the movements of settlers in America after the first comers had begun to scatter out beyond the seaboard constitutes a considerable handicap for anyone who would learn something definite about mixture of populations in this country. Add to this what any European would regard as the amazing laxity of local authorities in collecting vital statistics from immigrants—or anybody else—and you have some of the reasons why the blends in population in the United States may well impress the observer as being not so much separable strands as amalgams of which the original materials were thrown together so helter-skelter as to defy analysis. I believe that the editors of the American dialect atlas have found this situation, which prevails pretty generally throughout the country, a very serious drawback; and we need not therefore be surprised that Mr. Neely single-handed did not cope with it. In any case, he has given meticulously careful information as to the immediate provenience of his materials, and where the facts at his disposal have warranted he has speculated as to ultimate origins.

American folklorists, conversant with the situation to

which I have just alluded, will not expect to find here
data which they know can be found only with the
greatest difficulty if at all; they will rejoice to find not
merely a few waifs and strays of trans-oceanic traditions, but in addition a generous proportion of native
American materials—of folklore, that is, which has
arisen in America, and as such is part and parcel of the
spirit of America, that complex spirit, barbaric yawp
and all, of which one aspect has been adumbrated in the
paragraph just above. That this is genuine native folklore, unvarnished and unadorned, is so obvious in a
dozen ways that there is no need to stress the point. I
should like to direct attention to one conviction common
to many collectors from the days of the brothers Grimm,
a conviction fortunately not shared by Mr. Neely. That
is the conviction that unless we hurry, hurry, there
won't be any folklore worth collecting. The plain fact,
demonstrated over and over in the following pages, is
that folklore is always in the making, is always there to
collect when the right man comes along. People cannot
live without creating folklore, regardless of their envi-
ronment. Tenement children have their own games with
rhymes attached, games and rhymes which may be defi-
nitely different from the games and rhymes of the children in the next block of tenements. We need not expect
to find in the United States very good examples of the
glamorous fairy-tales of princesses in durance vile, but
we can expect to find tales of electric lights gone bad
and of automobiles come to grief through black magic,
through "hexing," of aeroplanes as curative agents, of
radios bewitched—indeed, what radio is not?—to name
only a few subjects which would seem least likely to live
in the lore of the folk according to the romantic ideas of
folklore as epitomized in "old, unhappy, far-off things,"
magic casements on the foam, and the like. Very little

of this ancient matter will be found in these pages, but the kind of folklore that is always with us awaiting the skilful collector is here in abundance.

Although the folklore of the southern fourth or fifth of Illinois has not been collected before, two other regions in or near Illinois have very recently received attention from collectors. I have asked Mr. Internoscia to show on the maps the two regions concerned. One, Adams County, Illinois, not much more than one hundred miles northwest of East St. Louis, provided materials for a book of some seven hundred pages and eleven thousand items, in 1935.* The other, Old Mines, Missouri, a village less than seventy miles southwest of East St. Louis and only thirty miles as the crow flies from Monroe County, Illinois—in "Egypt"—gave us seventy-three folk-tales in Creole French in 1937.†

With these works already accessible, with the establishment of the Southern Folklore Quarterly in 1937, with the probability that the Federal Writers' Project will soon be publishing selections from its collectanea in folklore, we may be entitled to suspect that the nineteen thirties and forties may one day be noted as marking a time when America's consciousness of its own folklore began to spread beyond the interests of a few scattered collectors. Perhaps this will be regarded as another symptom of America's coming of age.

These tales and songs I have felt bound to leave precisely as they were prepared by Mr. Neely. The usual small details of editing for the press I have carried out faithfully. An occasional note in the manuscript in the hand of Professor J. W. Ashton has been included, with

* Folk-lore from Adams County, Illinois, by Harry Middleton Hyatt. New York, 1935 [Memoirs of the Alma Egan Hyatt Foundation].

† Tales from the French Folk-lore of Missouri, by Joseph Médard Carrière. Evanston and Chicago, 1937 [Northwestern University Studies in the Humanities No. 1]. Earl J. Stout has published *Folklore from Iowa*, New York, 1936 [Memoirs of the American Folk-lore Society xxix.]

the addition of his initials. Professor Ashton showed great interest in the collection as it was being formed, and it is fitting that this enduring monument to Mr. Neely's persevering interest for many years should stand dedicated as planned.

J. W. S.

Evanston,
February 28, 1938.

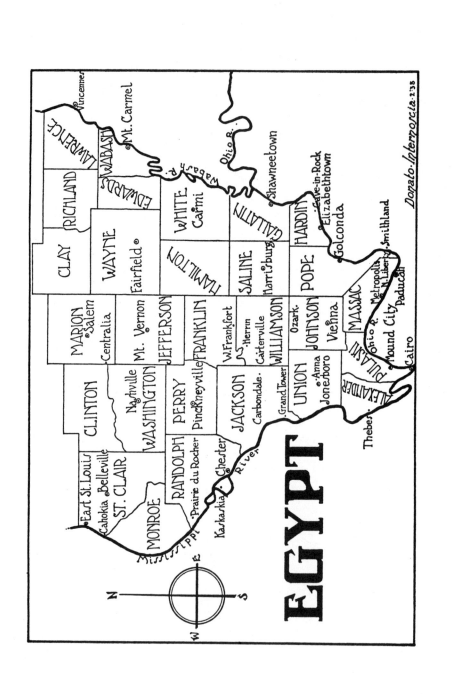

EGYPT

Donato-Intermozcia. 2:38

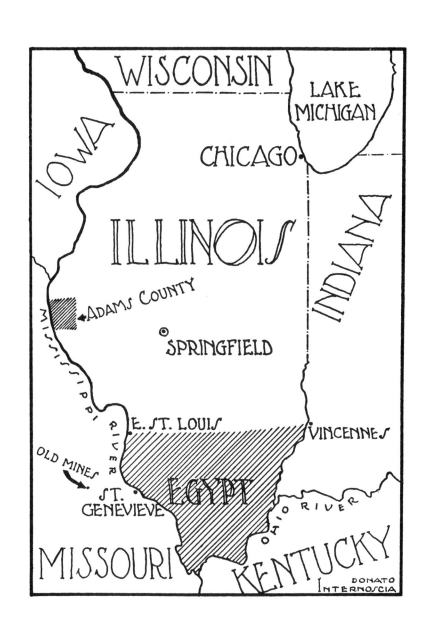

PART I

FOLK TALES

CHAPTER I

EGYPT

EGYPT IS the popular name of Southern Illinois. According to tradition, the people of the prairie land to the north gave it this name in the early days when a drought forced them to drive south for corn. They referred to these trips as "going down to Egypt." To this day, that section of Illinois which lies south of the tier of counties extending from Vincennes, Indiana, to East St. Louis, Illinois, is known as Egypt. Three of her towns actually bear Egyptian names: Karnak, Thebes, Cairo.

In topography, Egypt differs greatly from the rest of the state. Along its northern limits, prairie gives way to rolling hills which rise gradually to the foot-hills of the Ozark Mountains. Early settlers found these hills heavily forested, and enough timber still remains to give color to the landscape. Agriculture is the chief industry; the hills, as a rule, are set in apple or peach orchards or used as grazing land. Rich coal-deposits in those counties that mark the division between the prairie and the Ozarks have made Egypt one of the important coal-mining regions of the nation. Coal-mines have tempered somewhat the rural character of the section, attracting to the mining towns farmers and immigrants from Southern Europe. Towns, however, are still small, and the greater number of them are supported by agriculture.

The French were the first white settlers in Egypt. In the early part of the eighteenth century they established Kaskaskia and Cahokia in the American Bottom, which lies along the Mississippi River south of East St. Louis, in St. Clair and Randolph counties. The French and Indian War put an end to the French immigration,

3

and these settlements never became very populous.

Before the tide of later immigration the French quickly sank to a subordinate position. Today they are overshadowed, even in the American Bottom, by the descendants of American settlers and German immigrants. Those living on Kaskaskia Island are completely submerged and lead the shiftless lives of exploited tenant farmers, working no more than is necessary to keep body and soul together and clinging stubbornly to the past. Their conversations abound in references to George Rogers Clark, Pierre Menard, and the destruction of old Kaskaskia by the Mississippi River. Little of importance has happened to them in recent times. Separated from the rest of the state by the main channel of the river, the Kaskaskians are forgotten by most people and scorned by their thrifty and prosperous German neighbors. They are, however, the victims of unfortunate circumstance: an absentee landlordism robs them of an incentive to industry, and a rich alluvial soil makes it possible for them to live with little effort. On the main land, under happier economic circumstance, French of the same stock have matched their thrifty German neighbors in wealth and position. In Prairie du Rocher, for example, people of French descent are among the most prosperous and most prominent citizens.

After the American Revolution, as a result of Col. Clark's campaign across Southern Illinois, the territory was opened to American settlers. They came chiefly from North Carolina, Kentucky, Tennessee, and Virginia and were largely Scotch-Irish and English in descent. From them the great majority of Egyptians have descended, and their social and cultural pattern, distinctly Southern in character, prevails generally in this section.

In Randolph and St. Clair counties, however, German influence is strong, for those counties have been settled chiefly by German immigrants, who came in the thirties and forties of the last century. Today that region seems more like a detached portion of Germany than a part of Egypt. Many of the people are bilingual, speaking a broken English and a patois that is a strange compound of German and English words—a patois that is as incomprehensible to a master of literary German as it is to the English-speaking Southern Illinoisans. They keep their language alive in parochial schools, and they hand their folk heritage down from generation to generation. They tell German folk tales and sing German ballads and songs; they build houses that are decidedly German in architecture, quite the most distinctive in Egypt. Their towns are clean and trim and prosperous-looking; their farms are well-kept and thrifty in appearance, with sturdy buildings in the same style that prevails in the towns, more attractive usually than one finds in Egypt.

In spite of a sentimental attachment to their fatherland, manifested in their architecture, their folk literature, and their folk ways, these people worship at the same shrines as most Egyptians. One finds there the same devotion to progress as in other towns of Egypt, the same quota of boosters, sloganeers, and professional patriots, who are determined to save the land from radicals.

With the development of the coal-mines, hundreds of Italians and Slavs came into Egypt and settled in the coal-fields. Such towns as Benton, West Frankfort, Herrin, Du Quoin, and Harrisburg have large south European populations. Separated from native Egyptians by language, manners, and customs, they find it difficult to adjust themselves to a strange social and cultural pattern. As a consequence, they tend to congregate in certain sections of the mining towns and to live apart from the community—a situation which breeds racial prejudice. In spite of this segregation, these people find it impossible to preserve their cultural heritage beyond their own generation. Under the influence of the public schools, their children become much like those of their American neighbors. But unfortunately they lose their folk heritage without acquiring the folk heritage of the English-speaking Egyptians. They become as a result rootless individuals, less provincial perhaps in their outlook and less attached to Egypt than the children of native parents, but restless and maladjusted.

Although French, German, Italian, and Slavic people form a considerable part of the population of Egypt, they are after all minority groups, noticeable perhaps because of their difference from the majority of Egyptians, the descendants of the settlers from the Southern states. These Egyptians betray their Southern ancestry in a number of ways: in their speech, in their friendliness, in their easy-going ways, in their clannishness, in their racial prejudices (particularly against Negroes), and in their love of oratory, whether it be on the political stump or in the pulpit. An Egyptian is likely to feel more at home in Kentucky and Tennessee than he is in Northern Illinois, for his folk heritage is largely derived from those states. His ancestors brought many of his folk tales, most of his ballads and songs, and practically all of his superstitions from those states.

So strong was Southern influence that shortly after Illinois was admitted to the Union, Egypt almost voted slavery into the state. At the outbreak of the Civil War, lines were closely drawn in Southern Illinois between the Union and the Confederacy. Williamson County seriously considered an ordinance of secession. Many Egyptians fought in the Confederate Army; Captain Cunningham, John A. Logan's brother-in-law, raised a company at Shawneetown and led it South. General Logan was responsible, in a large measure, for the loyalty of Egypt to the Union. Neighborhood strife was common throughout the war, aggravated by the activities of the Knights of the Golden Circle, an organization of Southern sympathizers.

These early settlers from Southern states brought with them a tendency to clannishness, which the mountainous nature of the country has kept alive to the present day. Civil War passions took root in this clannish spirit and broke forth into feuds, the most famous of which was the Bloody Vendetta of 1874–1876 in Williamson County. In this feud three Republican families were aligned against three Democratic families. More than a dozen men were killed and wounded before the vendetta was finally stamped out. As recently as forty years ago the Arnett and Stanley families of Johnson County, which is one of the most isolated sections of Egypt, engaged in a feud that cost a number of lives. To this day, the neighborhood in which they lived is known as Hell's Neck. This clannishness nowadays betrays itself in milder forms—in a fairly strong local patriotism, in a deeply ingrained provincialism, and in a distrust of outsiders.

Strongly individualistic by nature, Egyptians have been prompt to assume the responsibility of law enforcement when constituted authorities have failed. Such failure led to the Regulator-Flathead Feud of Pope and Massac counties before the Civil War. The struggle, basically, was a question of the protection of property, though before it was over personal enmities aggravated the situation. The Flatheads, who lived in the river-bottom, had engaged in such illegal activities as counterfeiting, stealing stock, and murdering; they became so bold as to take teams away from boys working in the fields, and to drive off stock in broad daylight after changing marks. Finding officials unable to suppress these outlaws, the law-abiding citizens organized, whipped the Flatheads in a battle not far from Brookport, and lynched some of the leaders. But the counties were plunged into anarchy, and the militia had to be called out to restore order.

Labor trouble in the coal fields has often led to strife. In most cases the operators have been responsible, for they have attempted to break strikes by importing non-union workers. Such a policy invariably leads to bloodshed. Carterville was the scene of a race riot when Negro strike-breakers were brought in to work the mines during a strike. The same cause was responsible for the Lester Mine Massacre near Herrin shortly after the World War. During the summer of 1932, strife within the miners' union, between the rebel Progressives and the United Mine Workers, resulted in violence in Franklin and Saline counties. The struggle reached its climax in what is known as the Battle of Little Muddy River, in which the Franklin County sheriff and several hundred deputies turned back an invading caravan of miners and their wives, who were seeking to close the mines worked by the United Mine Workers.

Prohibition turned scores of Egyptians into moonshiners, for the country was well adapted to such an occupation. Moonshining led many Egyptians to join the Ku Klux Klan in an effort to enforce the Volstead Act. This organization, under the leadership of Glenn S. Young, plunged Williamson County into anarchy and left it the prey of two bootlegging gangs, one led by the Shelton Brothers and the other by Charlie Burger. These gangs fought for monopoly of the liquor traffic until the Sheltons were forced to retreat to East St. Louis, leaving Burger in undisputed possession of the field. Not until the death of Young in a spectacular gun-battle with Ora Thomas, deputy-sheriff of the county, the conviction of a state's attorney for conspiracy, and the execution of Burger for murdering the mayor of West City, was order restored.

This lawlessness and strife can be traced to such causes as protection of property, defence of jobs, Civil War enmities, and prohibition. Strife has never been general except during the Civil War, but its spectacular nature has made Bloody Williamson and Herrin household words and has given Egypt a bad name.

Egyptians have always taken a lively interest in politics, admiring particularly political orators of the old school. Their political thinking has never been daring; for the most part they are content to vote the Democratic or Republican ticket and have scant sympathy with radical parties and radical programs. They look rather to the past, regarding radicals with distinct hostility. Even the depression has failed to shake Egyptians from their traditional conservatism; it has only caused them to vote for Democrats when they would ordinarily have voted for Republicans, for Egyptians have been indifferent to the promises of a socialistic Utopia. Except for its rich coal-deposits, which have brought wealth to few Southern Illinoisans, Egypt is relatively poor in natural resources. Born and bred in poverty, Egyptians are reconciled to their narrow lives. Such economic development as they have enjoyed has been slow and modest; there has been no lack of boosters in the towns, with ambitious schemes to put Egypt on the map, but somehow their schemes have been barren in results. Farmers, especially in the hill sections, distrust such schemes and display little enthusiasm. What they want is less tax and a better price for corn and stock and fruit. When Republicans fail to deliver they vote in Democrats.

Turning again to the past, we find that the early settlers usually established themselves along the rivers—the French on the Mississippi, the Americans on the Ohio; gradually, settlements sprang up along the smaller streams, the Wabash, Kaskaskia and Big Muddy rivers, streams large enough for flatboats and later for small steamers. At first, the pioneers sent their produce by flatboat to New Orleans and obtained their imports from cities near the headwater of the Ohio. Later, steamboats changed the direction of trade, but flatboats did not disappear until recent times, though their importance steadily dwindled.

The era of the steamboat marked the dominance of such river towns as Chester, Grand Tower, Elizabethtown, Cairo, Mound City, Metropolis, Golconda, and Shawneetown, for they were the chief shipping-points and possessed flour- and lumber-mills. At Grand Tower there was an iron foundry, and at Mound City and Cairo during the Civil War were shipyards. Traveling men came by boat to the towns, and the hotels, generally built on the river-front, flourished as they have not done since. Showboats stopped periodically with their repertoire of *Uncle Tom's Cabin* and other melodramas. Excursion-boats with dance orchestras made frequent trips to points of interest up and down the Ohio and Mississippi. Deckhands chanted their songs as they loaded and unloaded cargo, and sometimes, under the influence of whisky, ran amuck. River-towns had the reputation, perhaps not wholly undeserved, of being wicked and immoral; certainly they were gay. But with the coming of the railroads the river-towns passed into decline. Today they suffer the inconvenience and now and then the disaster of high water without the compensating prosperity and gaiety of steamboat days.

Many stories have grown up about the river—stories of wrecks, of floods, of strong men, and of lawlessness. The most numerous and best-known of these stories concern the river-pirates at Cave-in-Rock, on the Ohio River, in Hardin County. At that town a cave extends some distance into the bluff along the river. This cave was the stronghold of pirates who plundered the flatboats that went down the river and murdered and robbed the returning flatboatmen and the settlers who crossed at Ford's Ferry a few miles above Cave-in-

Rock. The ferryman himself was in league with the pirates and with a villainous inn-keeper by the name of Potts, whose old inn still stands, a shunned and haunted building.

More accessible than the mountainous regions of Missouri and Arkansas, Egypt has changed in character more rapidly than they. Nowadays one finds little to remind one of pioneer times. Few of the log cabins are still standing; and towns, even the oldest ones—with perhaps the exception of Shawneetown, which still preserves its shabby antiquity—seem no older than the day of gingerbread woodwork. Almost alone of the towns of Egypt, Shawneetown lives in its traditions: the visit of La Fayette, the first bank in the state, and recollections of General Posey. Strangers are shown the general's battle-flag, a faded and moth-eaten emblem, kept securely behind glass in a local drug store; they are taken to see the Posey Building and are urged to visit the Posey grave. They are told how the bank refused to lend money to the founders of Chicago and how the Shawnee squaw kidnapped Dr. Reid's baby and left her own dirty papoose in exchange.

Manners and customs have changed; except in the more remote neighborhoods the young people seldom dance the old square dances, and the movies and the radio are rapidly driving out old ballads and stories as a means of enlivening winter evenings. Superstitions are dying out, though many of them still remain; any number of farmers sow and reap by the phases of the moon and geld their stock by the sign of the zodiac. The speech of Egyptians is fast losing its picturesque qualities as a result of the standardizing influence of public schools, movies, and radios.

In the hills the past still lingers on, in words and phrases suggestive of Elizabethan England and in manners and customs of an older day. Here and there, one still finds neighborhoods where people dance square dances and sing old ballads and songs to the accompaniment of stringed instruments. At Elizabethtown, Negroes and white people celebrate Emancipation Day, bringing their festivities to a close with a square dance. South of Carterville, in Williamson County, a farming community has a regular organization which meets weekly to play and sing ballads and songs from a manuscript book. These songs are usually of a mournful character, concerned with faithless lovers, murderous bridegrooms, repentant convicts and homesick exiles.

There is hardly a community, rural or urban, that will not yield to diligent search a number of tales and ballads. In the more industrialized sections their currency is somewhat circumscribed, radios and movies having taken their place with the majority of people, but even in such an industrial center as Belleville one finds a good many individuals who know both ballads and stories. In the hill sections, particularly in such counties as Pope, Hardin, Johnson, and Union, tales and ballads have a wider currency; in fact, they are the common property of a considerable portion of the inhabitants in the neighborhood. Ghost-stories appear to belong to certain families; usually these families are superstitious and tell the stories as if they had happened to a member of the family. Local legends are often family stories, too, telling, as a rule, the adventures of an ancestor or other relative. The best of these stories tend to become common property.

Although one may occasionally find a young person who remembers ballads and tales, generally the singers and narrators are old men and women, or at least middle-aged. A few inquiries will lead the collector to these individuals, for they have gained a local notoriety. Sometimes advanced age sets them apart from the rest of the community; often their ideas have earned them the reputation of being cranks; now and then a fickle versatility gains them the scorn of their more practical but less original neighbors; in a few cases shiftlessness ruins their standing. Usually, these story-tellers and ballad-singers are country people, or burghers with rural backgrounds. Many of them are superstitious enough to believe in the ghosts that they tell about and unsophisticated enough to be moved by the pathos of their songs. A few townsmen, interested in folklore as antiquaries, have made local collections.

Only to a sympathetic audience do these lovers of tales and ballad let down the reserve behind which they screen their interest from their workaday neighbors, for they have been too often the butt of good-natured contempt. Seldom will they admit their belief in ghosts, though they are convinced that they have received supernatural visitations, except among friends with like experiences. A filling-station operator at Elizabethtown expressed the prevailing attitude of most Egyptians toward these individuals: "Them old fools," he said, referring to certain story-tellers at Cave-in-Rock, "Have told them yarns till they believe they're so."

To the folk, their stories are spectacular and sometimes serious, and their songs and ballads are moving. Action in these stories and ballads is always objective, seldom complicated, and never subtle—such as appeals to the elemental emotions of unlettered people.

Stories dealing with the supernatural are more numerous in Egypt than those of any other kind. Of this type, by far the most common are concerned with apparitions; next in point of number are warnings. But one also finds stories of magic and transformation, generally of a human being to some animal. Closely allied to these are tales of gruesome death with a graveyard setting. Somewhat less numerous than supernatural stories are local legends, realistic stories of pioneer life, and Indian and outlaw tales. Practical-joke stories and tall tales have a fairly wide currency. Occasionally, one finds a variant of well-known European folk-tales; motifs common to those stories appear frequently.

The prevailing note in the ballads and songs is sadness. Some of the ballads are variants of Scottish and English ballads which appear in Child's collection; others are of American origin. A few are cowboy songs. Game-songs are relatively numerous, often existing in several variants. By far the most common song, however, is the doleful love-song, which tells of a love that was faithless or bereaved or crossed or murderous. Slightly less numerous are the songs of unhappy childhood: songs of motherless babes, of unloved orphans, of dying children, and of drunken fathers. A few songs and ballads are humorous, and now and then one finds a ballad that has been inspired by a local tragedy.

CHAPTER II

LOCAL LEGENDS

LOCAL LEGENDS are the most indigenous folk-tales found in Egypt, owing little, generally, to outside influences. Most of them spring from the experience of the pioneers, and many of them are historically true. Through these stories is refracted, not without distortion perhaps, a picture of folk life under primitive conditions. They show the pioneer in his relationship with the Indians and with the outlaws who menaced his life and property; they show him in his struggle with wolves and panthers; and they give us a glimpse into the concerns of his daily life. In them we get a vivid picture of Civil War enmities and the anarchic conditions which they bred. Many of these stories, possibly the greater number of them, are realistic, but some of them are romantic, one of them sufficiently so to engage the interest of journalists and local historians, who seem to have embroidered it out of all character.

Egypt has no legendary hero like Daniel Boone, David Crockett, or Paul Bunyan. John A. Logan is the nearest approximation to such a figure, but his appeal to popular imagination seems to be dying with the Civil War generation. Moreover, the folk hero was lost in the soldier and statesman. Had the late Big John Gentry of Cave-in-Rock lived at an earlier date, he might have grown into a folk-hero; his personality was vivid enough. But he died only a few years ago; in spite of that fact, however, he has become somewhat of a legendary character in Hardin County.

Very little of the Indian lore has been preserved; aside from the mounds, several of which have attracted the attention of archaeologists, there is little to suggest that this race ever inhabited Southern Illinois. The tribes were too weak to offer determined resistance to the encroachment of the white settlers. After the War of 1812 one hears less and less of them. The pioneers, however, acquired a number of their superstitions, learned a few of their simple remedies, and transmitted some of their stories. These stories have been preserved largely because they concern the white settlers in some way.

I

THE LEGEND OF TURKEY HILL[1]

The first white settlers came from West Virginia. They pushed westward down the Ohio to the Mississippi and up to East St. Louis. To the east they noticed a large, well-wooded, gently-sloping hill, and its height impressed them. There were many turkeys on this hill and they found that the hill was a resting-place for these turkeys on their migratory flights, and thus the name— Turkey Hill.

Because the land was in the shape of a horse-shoe, the settlers did not notice the Indians living there. The settlers, about twenty families, built their houses. They had quilting-bees and corn-husking parties. A shoemaker stayed with a family for a week and made the shoes for its members, and then went to the next house. The settlers carried their shoes and stockings until they came in sight of the church and then wore them. They were proud of their shoes and carried them in order to save them.

When the settlers discovered Indians on the hill, they expected trouble, but the Indians seemed friendly, and oddly enough they stood in awe of these white settlers who carried rods holding fire and thunder. The Indians told them how to fertilize and plough advantageously and gave them seed to plant. But the settlers noticed something strange about the Indian village. There were many old men and women and many squaws and children but very few braves. And these braves, strange to say, were maimed and crippled and horribly scarred and were no help for protection. The leaders asked the chief the reason for this and this is the story the chief told:

Years before, the Tamaroa Indians had a large town on Turkey Hill. They painted their faces, danced their war-dances, and made war on the other tribes of St. Clair County and the adjoining counties. They were always successful and came home victorious. Of course, they were greatly feared by the other tribes. One day in early spring, an elderly Indian appeared on Turkey Hill. He passed the sentinels quite mysteriously, and no one knew from whence he had come. He was tall and dignified with a goodly appearance and commanded respect. And strangely enough he carried no weapons, only a peace-pipe with a strange insignia. He asked permission to speak around the campfire. The Indians came to the meeting; even the women and children were permitted to stand in the background. The stranger told them that the Great Spirit wanted them to take up farming and to kill wild animals instead of Indians. The old man gave them good advice, telling the Tamaroas to be peaceful and never to go to war. As long as they obeyed this counsel they would be happy and have long lives, but if they disobeyed they would be punished. The Indians agreed to till the soil and stop their warfare. The stranger gave them seed of good vegetables— corn, potatoes, and peas. The wise man stayed with them until fall, and then he disappeared as mysteriously as he had come. For several years the Tamaroas did well and were happy and prosperous and were not molested, but at last they disregarded the sage instruction. After a time the young braves grew tired of this life, for deer-hunting seemed to be their only pastime. The young braves, at first secretly and then openly, made ready to go on the warpath. The Indians watched in sadness and sorrow as they departed. For several weeks they did not notice anything. Then they saw several of their braves crawling back to the foot of the hill. Many had died; others were severely wounded and crippled, and some came home to die. From those who returned, the tribe got the story of their torture and defeat at the hands of the Shawnee tribe. And that was why there were so few braves left in the Tamaroa tribe.

2

THE RED DRESS[2]

One day while Dr. Reid was away from home on a call, a small band of Indians came by his house. Mrs. Reid had just finished washing and dressing her baby and was sitting on the porch with him. The Indians stopped at the well for water. The braves left as soon as they had drunk, but the squaws stayed to admire the white baby with his light curly hair and pretty dress. One of the squaws, a young woman, remained after the rest had gone. She had a dirty, straight-haired papoose on her back, who made a poor comparison with the Reid baby. She put her papoose on the floor and snatched up the Reid baby, remarking, "Me swap." And she ran after the other Indians as fast as she could. Mrs. Reid attempted pursuit, but the squaw was too fast for her. When the doctor returned he found his wife half-crazy and an Indian papoose lying on the floor. Dr. Reid had his wife bathe the child, curl his hair, and dress him in the brightest dress that she could find. Then the doctor and his wife followed the Indians. When they reached the camp, the squaws crowded around them to admire the papoose, except the one with the Reid baby. She kept away. But soon she, too, came to admire the papoose. Once again she began to compare the babies, and this time the advantage was with her own child. She handed Mrs. Reid the white baby and took her own, remarking again, "Me swap."

*   *   *

Though Indian stories are somewhat scarce, there is no lack of animal stories. These tales seem to be factual accounts of the adventures of early settlers at a time when it was unsafe to venture out after dark unarmed. Very seldom are these stories irrational; the adventures seem to have been thrilling enough in themselves. When the irrational element is present, one feels that it is the result of a fairly common impulse to embroider the narrative. Stories of reptiles, however, are likely to have an irrational coloring.

3

THE CHASE[3]

John Gillespie's brother James and his sister, Abijah Neely's wife, lived in the same neighborhood. John was at his brother's home one evening, but he intended to go to his sister's to spend the night. James told him that it was dangerous. John didn't know much about animals and he insisted on going.

It was pitch dark when he left the house. There was no road, only a path that followed the ridge. Soon John was conscious that something was following him. He increased his speed. It wasn't long before he knew that he was being followed by a pack of wolves. He began to run. The rail fence that barred the way he took at a leap. The wolves leaped over on either side of him. As he neared his sister's house, he yelled to his brother-in-law to open the door. The wolves were snapping at him as he dashed into the house.

Another time John was making the same trip. This time he carried a half-burned piece of wood. As he swung the wood the fire would glow. He felt that some animal was near. He swung the brand a little farther back and it hit the nose of an animal. It gave a terrific scream and bounded off into the woods. He always thought that it was a panther that was about to spring.

4

THE WOMAN IN THE WOODS[4]

John Gillespie and his nephew started to visit relatives who lived in Illinois; at that time he was living in Kentucky. They came to Berry's Ferry, where most people who came into that part of the country crossed the Ohio River. It was growing dark, and the woods were thick on both sides of the river. The ferryman lived on the Illinois side. They holloed to the ferryman and a woman answered back in the woods. Gillespie yelled again and the woman answered. In the meantime the ferryman was well on his way across the river. Gillespie and his nephew talked the matter over and decided that they wouldn't go into the woods until the ferryman had landed. Again he yelled and again the woman answered. She was getting closer. He continued to yell at intervals and the woman always answered. She seemed to be getting nearer rapidly. The ferryman at length landed.

"There's a woman lost back in the woods," Gillespie told the ferryman.

"How do you know?" asked the ferryman.

"She's been yelling."

"Yell again."

Gillespie yelled again and she answered back in the forest at no great distance.

"Get in this boat in a hurry! That's a panther and it ain't very far away."

The two men rode back on the ferry and the ferryman began his return trip without loss of time.

5

THE PANTHER SCARE[5]

It was along in the winter. The snow was on the ground. The whole country was afraid; especially the women and the children was afraid to go to a neighbor's house. A panther was prowlin' around, an' its scream sounded like a woman screamin'. They saw its tracks where it had jumped twelve or fifteen feet. The whole country got aroused. They wanted to kill the panther. They got the best dogs in the country, but they couldn't get them to track it. The dogs was afraid. Then they got all the men together in that country an' had a general hunt. Now, this took place about three miles west of Cobden, where the panther had been comin' out of the bluff. Then it would go over this neighborhood. They all went around through the woods an' hunted all day an' never seen a thing of it. An' so they broke up about the middle of the afternoon, an' my old uncle, Madison Ring, was goin' home. An' as he was goin' through the woods, they saw the panther an' they's both scared. An' Madison Ring pulled off his hat an' shook it an' screamed an' run at the panther, an' it got scared an' run. An' it didn't come around the neighborhood any more.

One day another uncle of mine was goin' through a field to work, an' he seen the panther goin' along the bluff. He went back to his house an' got his rifle, an' took a short-cut on it, an' he killed it. She had four young ones in the bluff, an' she turned out to be a wolf.

6

ROBBING A WOLF DEN[6]

I used to work fer a feller named George Cummins. One Saturday evening he was out shootin' fish. He had his dog along, and the dog got snake bit. He just left the dog there, but Sunday mornin' he says, "Let's go back and see about the dog." We went back to where the dog was, and we seed that something had had a hold of him George said, "There's a wolf den here. A wolf's had hold of that dog."

We got to lookin' around, and we come to a cave where the dirt was dug up. We looked in and we seed an old she-wolf down on her paws, lookin' at us. A rock had been pulled off from above the cave, and there was a smooth place. We jumped up there, and as we jumped up a wild turkey flew off. It like to scared me to death. The turkey had been nestin' there.

We stayed there a long time. Finally, the old wolf come a-creepin' out like she was scared to death. She was a-goin' out to get the he-wolf. George, he sent me and my cousin to the house fer his gun. We had to go through a thicket. The old she had went out and found the he out there. I seed them first, but I didn't want to say anything, fer I knew my cousin would want to run, and he could run faster than I could. But finally he saw them. I said, "Let's git out our knives and fight them if they come after us." He said, "No, let's run." The old he-wolf grabbed hold of a post oak bush and bit it clear off. That scared us up some more, and we started to runnin'. My cousin got about ten feet ahead of me, and I says, "Hold on there. Don't run off and leave me." He slowed up.

The wolves didn't foller us, and we got the gun and come back to the cave. We set there all day, but the wolves wouldn't come up to the cave. They'd come up close enough fer us to hear them, but we never could catch sight of them.

Then Cummins says, "There's pups in there. You crawl in and get them." And I says, "The old wolf may be in there." And he says "I know she's not. I've been settin' here watchin' this cave." He got down to defend the path and keep the wolf from comin' in, and I crawled back in the cave. I crawled 'way back till I got where I could crawl no farther. I put my hand out in front of me, and I felt young wolves, I took them all out and petted two of them.

They finally killed the she-wolf. She was a big gray wolf. She measured nine feet from the tip of her nose to the tip of her tail.

I put my two wolves in a pen. Whenever I'd catch a rabbit I'd throw it to them. They'd fight to see which would git it. The winner would git the rabbit, and the one that was whipped would set off in a corner and look on while the other one et the rabbit.

One time a show come to town, and a showman offered me ten dollars fer my wolves, and I sold them.

*   *   *

Certain of these local legends are characterized by a homely realism, often spiced by a rude though healthy wit. They deal with such things as the experience of two men who went to Shawneetown to buy land on a slender purse, with the disappearance of a fat hog, with a man's killing his dog to get a coin, and with the theft of a dressed hog. In these stories one often perceives a thrift that comes of narrow economic circumstances; such thrift is usually amusing to the narrator, who frequently plays up the humor in his method of telling the story.

7

SOW BELLY AND CORN DODGER[7]

After the Mexican War Uncle Sam was hard up. He had a lot of company, too, for nearly everybody in the country was in the same fix. Uncle Sam needed some cash; so he cut the price of his land. He sold it at twenty-five cents an acre. Two men who lived in the country, Old Man George Elkins—he's almost become a historic figure now—and Evans Johnson decided to enter some land. At that time the land-office was in that old stone bank building at Shawneetown, and the way to get there was afoot. All this country was set in heavy forest—fine timber.

Money was scarce then. Everybody was hard up, along with Uncle Sam, but George and Evans managed to scrape up enough money for their fees. George had a little more than enough to pay his fees; his father-in-law gave him some money, but Evans just had enough for his fees. They took a little sow belly and dodger cornbread, and they carried a knapsack along for their commissary department.

When George and Evans got to Shawneetown they found that somebody else had heard about the cheap land, for the land-office was swamped with men wanting to enter land. The men at the land-office tried to find out some way to handle all the business as soon as possible. They finally decided to line the men up along the river bank. It made a line about a mile long. Every man had to hold his place. If he stepped out of line he lost his turn as you do in the barber shop. They would build a fire and cook their meat, and when night came they would lie down right there and sleep.

It was along in April about the time we have so many rains, and the men had nothing to protect them. Their bread got wet and soured, and their meat gave out, for most of them hadn't come prepared for a siege.

Men who had a little money besides their fees got along all right, and they could buy their food. George was fortunate. He had some money, and he didn't suffer much. But Evans just had enough for his fees, and he had to eat his soured bread and sow belly.

It took about ten days for George and Evans to get to the office, and in the meantime Evans had eaten up his meat and bread. He was about starved to death. By the time he was ready to start home, he was so weak he could scarcely make the trip.

8

THE LOST HOG[8]

I'll tell you a hog story. It must have been sixty or sixty-five years ago. In this country there were various opinions as to what a refugee was. One woman asked if "refugee" didn't mean a hundred days' thief. My folks were refugees. They came here in '65. Refugees had a hard lot; they were usually destitute. Of course, there were good and bad people among them, but they all had a hard time living. They came here with practically nothing. People were suspicious of them. Everything that they had to buy was high, and money was about as scarce as hen's teeth. Flour was twelve dollars a barrel and meat was sixty cents a pound. Poor people didn't do much buying. In those days everyone let his hogs run in the woods, and they'd get fat on acorns and nuts. There was plenty of game in the forests. Wild turkeys were still plentiful; so no one had to do without something to eat.

We moved out here, and Father took up some land along with another family that had come from the South. They built two log cabins and joined them with a hallway. And our families lived there. We had a neighbor who lived not far away. They didn't exactly know what a refugee was. The little boy of the family used to shy at us children when he passed along going to school. But finally he stopped and began to play. After that he played with us the same as he did with other children. Finally his mother came over, and she got to be a good friend of ours. She told us when we had become friends that her son had said that we were no different from any people even if we were refugees.

The man of that family had a good many hogs. One was a very fat fellow. Father had bought timber land when we came here. Trees were very large then. We had enormous poplar trees six and seven feet through. When it was blown over, a big poplar tree with a hollow place at the base would be large enough for a hog-house. Father had an old poplar tree that had fallen over on his place, and this man's hogs, among which was the fat hog, took to bedding in that tree.

The fat hog disappeared. The man got out to looking for it, for it was valuable, with meat at sixty cents a pound. The man would come to our house every once in a while and ask if we'd seen the hog. It looked kind of suspicious. There was Father's family and his friend's family living there and in need of everything, and the hog had disappeared on our land. There wasn't any trace of him anywhere.

About two or three months later, Father was out in the woods, and he saw a lean, lanky hog come wobbling down the path in the direction it would come if it was coming from the old poplar tree. It was the hog that had disappeared. Couldn't anybody solve the mystery of what had become of the hog.

The next year Father got hold of some hogs, and they bedded in the same old poplar, and one of them disappeared. Father looked everywhere, but he couldn't find the lost hog. One day he was out in the woods close to the old poplar, and he heard what he thought was the grunt of a hog in that hollow log. Father sent me home for an ax, and he cut the log open. There was the hog fastened up in that log. There was an opening up a way, but the passage was too narrow for the hog to squeeze through. Some night the hogs had crowded this one up that passage, and he had seen the light from this other hole and had tried to get out. A hog will live a long time on the fat he has put on.

That explained what had gone with our neighbor's hog, but it looked mighty suspicious with two refugee families that didn't have all the necessities of life. But the second hog cleared up the mystery.

9

THE TEN-DOLLAR GOLD PIECE[9]

Ole Jeff Ury, he carried an ole brown umbrella for years. He was a big, tall feller, very peculiar, a kind of odd feller, but a good man. His dog swallered a ten-dollar gold piece, an' it got out over town. He'd taught the dog to ketch things, an' he'd pitch up a coin, an' the dog caught it. An' he said he's afraid somebody'd kill the dog an' git the money, an' he killed the dog hisself an' got the coin.

10

THE HOG THIEF[10]

I had a brother that lived in Perry County. One fall he had a neighbor to help him butcher hogs. It took all day, and the man brought his wife along to help out. My brother had one hog that was extry big. It wasn't very cool then; so my brother decided to let the big hog hang by the gamboling sticks till morning. My brother said that he wasn't afraid of the dog bothering the hog.

The next morning my brother got up and milked and done all the work. He thought that it was about time for his neighbor to come over to help him cut up the hog. He looked down the field and saw a man. He separated the milk and looked down the field again, and there the man was, still standing in the same place.

My brother called his son Guy and told him to go with him. When they got down to the fence where the man was they saw that he had been carrying the big hog off. He had rested the hog on the fence, and it had slipped, and the gamboling stick had caught his neck, and the hog jerked him to the fence and killed him.

They called in the neighbors to look at the man, and they sent for the kurriner, so they'd be in the clear.

My brother's name was Allen Crashaw, and the thief's name was Jim Sorles.

*   *   *

Kaskaskia has been the scene of the most romantic legends of Southern Illinois, and the history of the town itself has been romantic—romantic and tragic. There at the mouth of the Kaskaskia River the French made their first settlement in Illinois, and on the hill above the site of the old town they built one of their strongest forts. At Kaskaskia, French explorers stopped and trappers brought their year's supply of furs. Kaskaskia was the objective of Clark's little army. It was near that town that Pierre Menard lived, and in the cemetery Shadrack Bond, the first governor of Illinois, was buried. The territorial government was there as well as the first capital of the state. With the removal of the capital to Vandalia, the decline of Kaskaskia began. Later the county seat was moved to Chester, and near the turn of the last century the Mississippi, changing its course, washed Old Kaskaskia away, and today the river flows over its site. Such a history would tend to make legends romantic.

I I

ADRIFT ON THE MISSISSIPPI[11]

A priest came to Kaskaskia one time.[12] In those days everything that was done was sworn to before the priest at the altar of the church. One time some people wanted to swear to something that was not true before the priest. Most likely they were Americans that didn't belong to the Catholic Church. The priest knew that it was a lie, and he wouldn't let them swear to it. This made them mad, and they seized him and put him in a canoe and set him adrift on the river. When he was drifting away he put a curse on the town to the fourth generation. And sure enough Kaskaskia was washed away. But now the curse ought to be lifted because this is the fourth generation. Sometimes folks say it was an Indian that people didn't like that was set adrift in a canoe. They didn't want the Indian there. And he put a curse on the town.

I 2

LA FILLE[13]

Rosalie Antaya married an Italian that came to Kaskaskia. He was a trader. One time he wanted her to swear to something that was untrue, and she refused. He said that he would leave her if she didn't. She told him to go ahead. And she walked with him down to the river. He got in his canoe and asked her if she was going to swear. She told him that she wasn't. She said for him to wait and she would give him a push. He said that he was leaving because he loved her and she wouldn't do what he wanted her to do. She gave his boat a push and he left. She told him never to come back because she had a lot of friends among the French and Indians. He never came back. She brooded over his leaving until she lost her mind. She thought that she was a girl again and called herself la fille.

13

THE BUSS[14]

I can tell you a real story about the Civil War. My grandfather, Joshua G. Burch, sympathized with the South, and when Southern soldiers came along, he took them in and hid them. He would let them rest and then send them along. One time a Confederate soldier came along in disguise. He was a stranger. My grandfather took him in. Folks found it out some way, and the officers came to arrest J. G. Burch. They took him to the home of a man named Clark on the other side of the river near Prairie Du Rocher. They promised to let Burch stand trial, but they were going to kill him. He found it out from one of the girls who was waiting on the table.

Grandfather was always full of fun. He told the girl that she was so pretty that he wanted to give her a buss. (He always said buss for kiss.) She found out that they were going to kill Grandfather on the bluff not far off. She told the officers that she wouldn't wait on them if they didn't take their guns off because they made her nervous. They took off their guns and laid them down on the floor and put a man to guard Grandfather, who was in a room. The men had a good dinner and they forgot about their prisoner, for they were having a good time.

The apron that the girl wore had a big pocket, and she stole a gun and hid it in the pocket. They didn't notice because she flirted with the officers. She managed to steal the key to the handcuffs, too. Then she slipped to the room that Grandfather was in. She unlocked the handcuffs and gave him the gun and told him that there was a horse in the field.

As Grandfather had one leg through the window, he turned around and kissed the girl. She said to him, "Go on, you fool!"

He said, "I'm no fool. I've just kissed the prettiest girl in the country."

He got away and went home. Then he sent word to the officers to come and get him, but they never bothered him.

*   *   *

The next two stories are not Kaskaskia stories, but they seem to have much the same romantic coloring. The scene of the first one is Dug Hill, a pass through a steep hill, cut by the pioneers, five miles or so west of Jonesboro, to give an outlet to the river. Like the last story, this one deals with the Civil War. The scene of the second story is Kentucky along the trail that led from Berry's Ferry to Franklin.

14

EXECUTION OF AN INFORMER[15]

When Lincoln was a-runnin' for President, he didn't say anything about freein' the slaves, but after he got in office he took a notion to free the niggers, and he did in 1863. A lot of the Democrats that were in the Union Army didn't want the slaves freed, and after Lincoln issued his proclamation they begin desertin' the army. Union County was filled with deserters. Some of them went up into Canada, but most of them hid out in the woods of Union County. The deserters always carried their shootin'-irons with them, for they didn't know when they'd meet soldiers or officers. They hid out in the woods most of the time. Most of them slept there and in barns. Sometimes they killed game and cooked it, but most of the time they'd hide out close to home. The womenfolks would hang out white rags at a place designated to signal the deserter that the coast was clear, and he'd slip home and get something to eat and slip back to the woods. I'd a lot rather stay in the army than to live in the woods, scared at ever stick that cracked or ever time the wind rustled the leaves.

The Government sent a man into the country to hunt these deserters down and arrest them. He was called a provost marshal. When he arrested a deserter he would take him to Cairo and turn him over to the military authorities. Certain men in the country would turn the deserters in to the provost marshal. They were called informers. The informer got thirty dollars for every man he turned in, but I don't know how much the provost marshal got. One time at Anna the provost marshal arrested three deserters. There was a big crowd of deserters collected there, and they took the three men away from him and would have killed the provost right there if some level-headed Democrats hadn't been present.

There was a man that lived over in the bottoms on the other side of Dug Hill named Welch, and he was an informer. He turned in deserters and got thirty dollars a man. It made a lot of men mad because he was a-tryin' to force men into the army and he didn't join the army hisself when the war began. Of course, the deserters was a-layin' for him. This man Welch turned in a lot of deserters, and he was dangerous because he knew where they hid.

A bunch of deserters—about ten or twelve of them— formed a plot agin Welch. One deserter pretended to be

Welch's friend, and he rode with him out toward Dug
Hill. The other men in the plot went on ahead. One of
them loaded the guns. He put blank cartridges in all
the guns but two, and then the men selected the guns.
They all hid in the bushes on top of the hill above the
pass. Welch had to pass right below them. The deserter
that was with Welch made some excuse to leave him
before they got to the hill. He said he had some business to attend to or something. Welch rode on and when
he got to the place where the men were hid, they fired
on him and killed him. Ever since then they say that
that neighborhood is hainted. People couldn't keep
their doors to when they locked them, and some people
have seen ghosts there.[16]

15

THE STRAYED HORSE[17]

This happened about 1830. John Gillespie was visit-
ing his sister in the Gooseneck, as the southern part of
Pope County was called. In that day both Kentucky
and Illinois were pretty wild; there were still panthers
and wolves and deer in the woods. On this visit John
bought a nice saddle-horse, that he paid one hundred
and fifteen dollars for. He rode his horse back home,
near Franklin, Kentucky, which is about one hundred
miles from the Ohio River.

Shortly after his return, the horse broke out and
started back to Illinois. Gillespie started after it and
traced it about sixty miles but couldn't catch it. In
the neighborhood of Nortonville, Kentucky, he lost
track of the horse: he could trace it to that neighborhood but no farther. He began to search the community
for his horse with disappointing results. Finally, he met
an herb-doctor who was digging roots and asked him

if he had seen anything of the horse. This doctor was
an old man. He told Gillespie that the horse was being
held at a country store not far away and that the man
who had it kept the horse hid by day. The herb-doctor
told Gillespie that he might inquire at the store, though
he didn't think that it would do much good.

Gillespie went to the store and asked if there was a
stray horse there. And he said that he had heard that
there was and that he wanted to see it. The proprietor
demanded to know who had told him and said that he
had no stray horse about his place.

Gillespie went back to the herb-doctor, who told him
that he would have to steal his horse if he ever got it
back. The doctor told him to go to his house and stay
hidden until night, for the horse was sure to come in
after dark. This Gillespie did. After dark when he
started out, the doctor told him to get his horse and
leave the country and that it wouldn't be best for him
to stop anywhere that night.

Gillespie rode to the store, stopping to hitch his horse
in the woods not far away. Then he went up to a hazel
thicket which was close to the store and waited. After
a while he heard his horse coming down the trail; he
recognized it by its gait. The rider came to the thicket
where Gillespie was hiding, jumped down, hitched the
horse, and went to the store to find out if any one had
been looking for the horse, just as the herb-doctor said
that he would do.

Gillespie didn't lose any time. He took the saddle and
bridle off the horse, fastened his halter on its head, and
led it back to the other horse. All that night he rode and
all the next day, without stopping, but no one followed
him.

*   *   *

Before the Civil War the inhabitants of Pope and
Massac counties were aroused to indignation by the
bold and daring theft of stock by certain families in the

Ohio Bottom. Unable to recover property by lawful means and to put an end to the robberies, people organized regulator bands and subdued these outlaws, who were called Flat-heads. But the regulator bands quickly became instruments to gratify personal grudges, and thus inaugurated a reign of terror which drove the Flat-heads to cooperate with state and county officials in an effort to restore peace. Enmities aroused by that conflict lasted for several generations.

16

THE VICIOUS STALLION[18]

The Flat-heads lived down in the Ohio River bottoms in Massac County. They would come up into the hills and steal cattle, hogs, and horses, and drive them off into the bottoms. In those days it wasn't safe to leave a boy plowing alone in the field, for some of the Flat-heads would come along and drive the team off. No one dared to go after his stock because he would never come back alive.

Mr. Weaver lived in the hills a mile or so north of New Liberty. He had a fine stallion, which the Flat-heads wanted, but they never could get it.

One morning Mr. Weaver saw that some one had been trying to steal his horse. That night he hid in the barn in the hay. Sure enough, along in the night, several of the Flat-heads came. They tried to get the stallion, but he was a vicious brute and fought them off. They took a rope and looped it and put it on the end of a stick and they tried again. Mr. Weaver saw that they were going to get the horse and he shot. One of the men fell. Two of the Flat-heads grabbed the fallen man and ran before Mr. Weaver could reload his gun, and Mr. Weaver was afraid to follow the men because he was alone.

17

BONES IN THE WELL[19]

When we first married, my husband and I lived with Hens Adkins south from New Liberty. One day Sary, Hens's wife, and I were cleaning up the house and we run across the picture of a young man. Sary looked so queer that I asked her what was the matter and she said she felt so bad about that young man. His name was Taylor and he had helped Hens make a crop one year. He had disappeared, leaving all of his clothes, and had never been heard of any more.

There were some black spots on the stair-steps and I asked Sary what caused them. She said they'd killed a hog and had taken it upstairs and some of the blood had got on the floor.

Sary's sister married a man by the name of Kelley. One day Sary got mad at Hens and she told her sister that Hens had killed Taylor. He had cut Taylor's throat while he was laying on a pallet. After he had killed the man, he made Sary help him carry the body upstairs. They left it up there a day and they took it out and put it in a straw stack. Hens set fire to the straw stack, but all the bones didn't burn up. So Hens gathered up all the bones and put them in a bucket with a wedge and an ax blade and sunk them in the well.

When we moved there, we were getting water from a well out by the barn. I noticed the well at the house and I asked Sary why we couldn't get water there and not carry it so far. She said the water in that well wasn't good because Hens never would clean it out.

Kelley didn't like Hens. One day when he caught Hens away from home, he cleaned out the well. He found the bucket just like Sary said it was. There was the wedge, the ax blade, and the bones. Kelley took the bones to New Liberty, but the doctor wouldn't say that they were human bones. Hog bones look a lot like human bones.

Hens just passed it off as a joke. He'd laugh and tell people how they tried to frame him.

*   *   *

One of the most interesting outlaw stories of Egypt concerns Jesse James. It is not a spectacular story, for it merely tells of a visit the notorious robber paid to a boyhood friend, a certain Jim Powell, who lived not far from New Liberty, Illinois. People in that section have delighted in the story partly because, like most hero-worshipers, they love to dwell upon the human qualities of their hero, but more because they have known personally or by report a man who had been reared in the same neighborhood as Jesse James.

18

A VISIT FROM JESSE JAMES[20]

Jim Powell lived across the river from Smithland, Kentucky, and about a mile north. He did nearly all of his trading in Smithland and was pretty well known there.

Jesse James and his gang had robbed a bank up at Danville, Kentucky. And they had separated after the robbery. Jesse came down to Smithland. No one knew him. One morning he heard some men talking about Jim Powell. He asked them if Jim Powell lived near, and they told him that he lived across the river on the Illinois side. James said no more, but he sauntered down to the river and hired a man to row him across the river to a place James indicated.

In the late afternoon a stranger stopped in front of Powell's home, which was in the river bottoms and surrounded by a dense forest. Powell went out and talked a while with the stranger, and then they both came in. Powell introduced the visitor as Mr. Taylor, a boyhood friend.

After supper Powell and Taylor went into a room to themselves and talked. Taylor sat near the window and he removed his belt and pistol, which he laid in the window within reach. When Mrs. Powell thought it was bed-time she came into the room and asked them if they weren't ready to go to bed, but they told her not to bother, that they would go to bed when they were ready. The two men talked all night, and the next morning Taylor left.

No more was said of the stranger who visited that night at Powell's. Mrs. Powell forgot about it, and Powell, who was always a close-mouthed man, never referred to it.

Several years later when Powell was on his deathbed, he called his wife to his room. "Do you remember the Mr. Taylor who stayed all night here?"

"Yes."

"That was Jesse James."

Powell and Jesse James had grown up in the same neighborhood and had been boyhood friends. When James had left Powell's home he had told Powell that he might tell Mrs. Powell who he was after his death. But Jesse James had been dead several years before Powell told the story.

*   *   *

Local legends give us a vivid, but by no means complete, picture of early days in Egypt; the significance of the picture lies in the fact that it is an intimate glimpse into the daily concerns of the common folk. They show us the white settlers living side by side with the Indians and braving the dangers of the forests infested with wolves and panthers. They give us realistic vignettes of daily life, often touched with humor. Some of them throw a glow of romance over the incidents of the past, particularly so in the case of the legends from Kaskaskia. They reveal to us the strife and enmity of Civil

War times, with its clash of divided loyalties and its distrust of Southern refugees. And they show us the lawlessness of early times before authority had firmly established itself. Here and there in the stories a single sentence quickens to life a past that has long been dead.

NOTES ON CHAPTER II

1. Miss Esther Knefelkamp, Belleville, gave me this legend. She obtained it from Miss Emilie Heber; also of Belleville. The story is known generally among individuals of antiquarian interests in Belleville, Freeburg, and the Turkey Hill neighborhood. It is not widely known in Southern Illinois and not very well known to people in general in St. Clair County, in which those places are situated. The tale was told by the Tamaroa Indians to account for their peaceful habits; it is one of the few Indian myths that has been preserved.

Turkey Hill, which is said to be one of the highest points in the county, lies between Belleville and Freeburg. It had served as a regular camping ground for the Tamaroas, who were still using it as such when the first white settlers came into that section before 1800. A Mr. Voelkel, who owns the farm on Turkey Hill, has found many Indian relics on his place and has given them to the Smithsonian Institution. He believes that his farm is a part of the old Tamaroa village.

2. Mr. Marsh Wisehart of Shawneetown told this version of the story. Almost every one in Shawneetown knows the story; while I was in that town I heard it told by two other people, one of whom was a descendant of Dr. Reid. The story seems to be more widely known in Egypt than most folk tales. I heard it first many years ago in Carbondale. In all of the versions with which I am familiar there is very little variation; the essential features remain the same. Sometimes the narrator makes the kidnapped baby a boy and sometimes a girl; sometimes he has the doctor take the papoose to the Indian camp, sometimes the doctor's wife, and sometimes both of them. But the kidnapping and the way in which the child is recovered remain the same in all versions.

3. This story and the one which follows, also narrating the adventures of John Gillespie, were told by Mr. Charles Neely, Sr., of Carbondale. The scene of Story Number 3 is the southern part of Pope County; that of Number 4 just across the Ohio River in Kentucky at Berry's Ferry. Both stories are family tales, with which I have been familiar from childhood, told only in my family, so far as I have been able to discover. Stories concerning John Gillespie were handed down by Matthew Neely, my grandfather, who was his nephew. Gillespie left no direct descendants, never having married, but he assumed the responsibility of providing for his sister and her family after the death of his brother-in-law, Abijah Neely. He seems to have been somewhat of a bold and daring man and, according to family tradition, somewhat of a gallant in his young days. Because of his gallantry, Story Number 4 excites good-natured mirth in the family.

4. See Footnote 3, above.

5. This story was written down from the lips of the late Isaac J. Hartline of Carbondale in his eighty-fourth year. Formerly, he had lived in Union County near the scene of this story. The tale is not widely known; apparently it was a family legend well on the road to oblivion. In the winter of 1928 when I secured this story, Mr. Hartline had not told it for a good many years.

6. Secured from Mr. John M. Harper, Ozark, Illinois, who was eighty years old at the time he told this story. He had a reputation as a story-teller, in Johnson County, often entertaining court-house loafers at Vienna, the county seat of Johnson County, with his stories. Consequently this story was fairly well known. In fact, the county superintendent of schools introduced him to me as a man who knew folk tales.

7. Mr. D. M. McCall of Buncombe, Illinois, told this story. It is fairly well known in and around Buncombe, partly because George Elkins was a wealthy farmer and had lived to be a hundred years old, receiving as a consequence a considerable amount of publicity.

8. This tale was secured from Mr. D. M. McCall of Buncombe, Illinois. It is a family legend, scarcely known outside the McCall family, who came as refugees to Southern Illinois during the Civil War. It shows vividly the plight of such families. Loyal Egyptians suspected their patriotism, and Southern sympathizers looked upon them as traitors to the South. Like the last story, this one was told in a humorous way, but here the humor is not inherent in the material, springing rather from the narrator's impulse of giving a funny turn to his story.

9. Secured from the late Isaac J. Hartline, Carbondale. See Note 5, above. The story is hardly more than an anecdote, but it is widely known in Anna and Jonesboro, Illinois. Ury's home was in Anna, and he seemed to have been a local "character."

10. Obtained from Mr. John Crashaw, Carbondale. The story is a family legend, at this date not very well known in the Crashaw family, for the younger generations have slight interest in tales of this sort. In the past, the Crashaws have been very careful with family records, but these records seem to have been factual accounts of marriages, births, deaths, locations of homesteads, etc. Apparently, the best story-teller in the family was Mr. Crashaw's grandmother, for most of his stories have come from her.

11. Obtained from Mrs. Mary Louise Garner, Kaskaskia, Ill. Mrs. Garner has heard this story from childhood. It is one of the best-known legends of Southern Illinois. Mr. Elbert Waller published a somewhat melodramatic version of the story in a booklet entitled *Illinois Pioneer Days*, E. B. Lewis, Litchfield, Ill. In his version the priest has become a Christianized Indian fur-dealer who elopes with Marie Benard, the daughter of a prosperous merchant. The father leads a posse in pursuit of the fleeing pair, chains the Indian to a raft, and sets him adrift and puts his daughter in a convent. The Indian curses the town, and on stormy nights his ghost floats over the site of Old Kaskaskia. The St. Louis *Globe-Democrat*, June 23, 1928, carries a feature story of the people of Kaskaskia looking for the lifting of the curse, and gives a version somewhat similar to the one above.

12. The priest was Father St. Cyr, who in 1833 was pastor at St. Louis. According to Father L. J. Garroghan, S.J., who has made a study of Father St. Cyr's pastorate in Chicago, Father St. Cyr was located at Kaskasia and across the river at Ste. Genevieve.

13. Secured from Mrs. Mary L. Garner, Kaskaskia, Illinois. The story is well known on the Kaskaskia Island.

14. Obtained from Mrs. Mary L. Garner, Kaskaskia. This is a family legend. Its circulation is restricted to the Garner and Burch families.

15. Obtained from the late Isaac J. Hartline, Carbondale. This story is well known in the Dug Hill Neighborhood, west of Jonesboro, in Union County. The chief reason for its being known so well is the fact that the murder of Welch brought into being the Dug Hill apparition. See Stories 45, pp. 75-77, and 48, pp. 80-81.

16. See Stories Number 45, pp. 75-77, and 48, pp. 80-81.

17. Told by Mr. Charles Neely, Sr., Carbondale. This is a family story, told apparently only in the Neely family. It is one of the tales that I have heard from childhood. Very possibly the story is told among the Neelys who live in Kentucky.

18. Secured from Mr. Charles Neely, Sr., who in his boyhood had lived in the same neighborhood as Mr. Weaver and was intimately acquainted with the latter's sons. The story was fairly well known a few years ago in the southern part of Pope County, for Mr. Weaver was one of the most prominent men in that section, serving as justice of the peace and keeper of the paupers. Apparently, the Flat-heads never returned to avenge their fallen comrade nor attempted to rob Mr. Weaver again. No one ever knew what really happened to the man who was shot, whether the wound was slight or fatal. The Flat-heads lived pretty securely in the bottoms, a wild and uninviting region. Few people dared venture into it, and the Flat-heads were very reticent about their confederates.

19. The late Mrs. Julia M. Bell, who lived in Carbondale in her old days, was the narrator of this story. Formerly, she had lived in Pope County, the scene of this story. A number of years ago the story was well known in the southern part of Pope County; it is only one of a number of tales concerning Hens. In his younger days, Hens had gained a certain local notoriety with his evil deeds. And the fact that he was a crippled man made him seem a sinister figure. In his old age he became religious, and many people remember him as a faithful church-goer, but he never lived down his evil reputation.

20. This tale was told by Mr. Charles Neely, Sr., Carbondale. It is well known in the southern part of Pope County. Mr. Neely knew Powell personally and described him as a man who had little to do with his neighbors. Powell seems to have been somewhat brutal; there is a well authenticated story of his chasing a number of school-girls, including a step-daughter, with his horse. He was not, however, connected with the James Gang, nor was he guilty of any unlawful acts. He lived the quiet and uneventful life of a farmer in comfortable circumstances.

CHAPTER III

HUMOROUS TALES

PRACTICAL jokes seem to be the most typical form of Southern Illinois humor; certainly more of its humorous stories are built on that pattern than on any other. Tall tales are perhaps next in popularity. Egyptian humor, as revealed in these stories, is rollicking, masculine, and rude, often arising from the discomfiture of some individual. For the most part, however, it is kindly; seldom is it satirical or ironical. The tellers of the humorous stories seek to arouse loud laughter, the louder the more successful the story; the subtle humor of irony or satire leaves most Egyptians a little perplexed. The spirit of David Crockett and of Mark Twain, in his less subtle moments, breathes through these stories.

In the first two stories of this group, the humor of the one depending upon a witty answer which happens to be broadly ironical and that of the other upon a pun, we have types rare in Egypt; they are almost never told by the folk.

19

SQUIRE BURGH ON THE LAW[1]

There was a man named Colonel Lawrence Hay who used to live in our community. When he was drunk he was the vilest and most vulgar man in the world, but when he was sober he was a perfect gentleman. He was a tall man—I should say about six feet one—and very dignified. He was handsome, well-bred, and cultured.

He used to try a good many cases before the J. P. courts. Of course, he wasn't a lawyer.

Col. Hay used to try cases before Squire Don Emmanuel Burgh, who lived not far away. Col. Hay and Don Emmanuel were sworn buddies. They used to drink whisky out of the same jug.

One day Col. Hay was trying a case before Don Emmanuel, and Don Emmanuel ruled against him every time. At length he overruled an objection of Col. Hay's that the latter knew was wrong. He got up and said, "Your Honor, such and such a law passed at a certain date settles the proposition in my favor."

"Col. Hay," said Don Emmanuel, "I have always made it a practice in trying cases to know as little about the law as possible."

"Don Emmanuel," said Col. Hay, "you have succeeded admirably."

20

DR. BOGGS'S PRAYER[2]

Old Dr. Boggs was pretty much of a "character"; he fairly ate tobacco and was soused most of the time. He was a rough-speaking old man. He stayed at a hotel. He had a room on the second floor. The porch of the hotel was only one story, and Dr. Boggs was in the habit of taking a chair and going out on the roof of the porch to sleep off his whisky.

One day they tore the porch away; they were going to build another one. The Doctor forgot about it, and, as usual, after dinner he got his chair and stepped out of the door. He said that just as soon as he made that step he realized that it was time to pray, but the only prayer he could think of was the blessing his father used to say: "Lord, we thank Thee for what the body is about to receive." The Doctor said he knew damned well that that prayer wouldn't do.

* * *

The next group of stories are tall tales. Usually, these stories contain such obvious exaggerations that they excite loud guffaws, but sometimes they are told with an apparent seriousness and with a straight-faced earnestness that deceive the casual listener. Acquaintances of the story-teller, however, are not deceived; they know that his tale is a big lie and are amused or indifferent, depending upon their characters. Part of the fun of these stories is the deception of an unwary listener. The first two stories are of this type; told with an effort to secure verisimilitude, they might lead a stranger to class them as true accounts of actual incidents, though perhaps exaggerated.

21

THE SNAKES AT SWAN'S POND[3]

This story I used to tell and the men would laugh at it. As long as so-and-so was alive he would stand up fer me, fer he was there. I'd get with a bunch of men in town and I'd see him a-comin', and I'd say, "so-and-so, come here. Is it the truth about them snakes down at Swan's Pond?" And he would say, "Yes, boys, it was the truth, just like John told it. I was there and I seed it."

One time some five of us went over to what we used to call Swan's Pond, out close to Simpson. We went deer-huntin'—it was in the spring of the year. The pond was all growed up in water bonnets, and they was a thicket all around it. The hounds got out there and went to barkin.' I said, "If it was me I'd kill them dogs fer barkin' that way." But the man that they belonged to said that they wouldn't be barkin' if they wasn't something there. I said to one of the fellers, "I'm gonna wade out there and see what it is." And he went along with me.

When we got there we seed a roll of snakes might near as big as a barrel. It was the purtiest sight I nearly ever saw. They was all kinds of color. I says, "I'm gonna shoot into that." He says, "No, don't you do it! Snakes will scatter in every direction." But I shot anyhow right through the roll of snakes. We didn't wait to see what would happen. We went a-runnin' to the bank. When we got to the bank we seed cotton-mouths on every dry place. Their mouths were open. You never seed a bunch of men run so in your life.

22

SNAKE OR DEVIL[4]

I'll tell you what I seed once, and it's always been a mystery. I never could account fer it. I had a field of clover on a hill one year, and I cut it one Saturday. Next Sunday mornin' I got on a horse and rode up to the field to see if it was dry.

As I was a-settin' there on my horse I seed the awful-lest snake that ever I saw. It was rared up about three feet. Its head was the shape of a heart. Its neck was bowed up, and its eyes looked like buck-shot. It was about fourteen feet long.

I looked and I looked. I tried to think what I could do. Directly I seed a big limb and got down off my horse and got it. When I looked up I couldn't see the snake anywhere.

I never told anybody about what I'd seed except my wife, fer it was too much of a snake-story. But sometime later my brother-in-law, that lived three-quarters of a mile across the creek, saw the same thing

I'd seed. He described the very thing I'd seed. I never could solve that thing. I know I weren't scared, fer I was on horseback. I never would have said a word about it if my brother-in-law hadn't seed it.

My brother-in-law and me talked about it a heap of times, and he said he didn't know what it could have been unless me and him were the only two men that was ever permitted to see the devil.

I know I wasn't scared. When I got home I called my dog and got my gun and went back. My dog would track a snake down if I'd take him where it had been, but he wouldn't track this one. I took him right to the place, and he just walked off.

23

THE DEEP SNOW[5]

Schiederhannas saddled his horse one day to take a ride to the court-house. After riding in a heavy snow-storm all day he found the court-house closed. And being weary and tired he stopped, got off his horse and tied his horse to what he thought was a hitching post. Then he took his blanket from his horse and spread it upon the snow and lay down on it and went to sleep. Awakening the next morning, he looked about for his horse, and to his amazement he saw that the snow was melted, and there was his horse tied to the cross of the church steeple. So he took out his pistol and shot off the strap with which his horse was tied. Down came the horse and Schiederhannas rode away.

24

OLD MAN BLOODWORTH'S MULES[6]

Old Man Bloodworth lived out near Cottage Home. The post-office there has been discontinued for many years. The Old Man had a team of mules that he was very proud of, and he boasted about what they could do. He said that when he went to town and it looked rainy it didn't worry him none. 'Cause when it started raining he would put the groceries in the front half of the wagon, and the rain would only fall in the back half of the wagon all the way home—that's how fast they were.

He also said they were very good at pulling a load and that he would have twice as much on his wagon as he should, and when they would come to a hill they would pull and pull till their bellies touched the ground. While they were pulling so they would look for rocks to hook their feet over to give them traction. When they couldn't find a rock, they would reach out with their teeth and grasp a sapling and pull themselves along.

25

THE CAT WITH THE WOODEN PAW[7]

Jack Storme was the local cooper and blacksmith of Thebes. He had a cat that stayed around his shop. The cat was the best mouser in the whole country, Jack said. He kept the shop free of rats and mice. But one day the cat got a fore-paw cut off. After that he began to grow poor and thin and didn't take any interest in anything because he wasn't getting enough to eat.

So one day Jack decided to fix him up a wooden paw. He whittled one out with his knife and strapped it on the maimed leg. After that the cat began to grow sleek and fat again. Jack decided to stay at the shop one night to see how the cat managed it with his wooden paw.

After dark the cat got down in front of a mouse-hole and waited. Pretty soon a mouse peered out cautiously. Quick as a flash the cat seized it with his good paw and knocked it on the head with his wooden one. In no time that cat had eighteen mice piled up before the hole.

*   *   *

Southern Illinois humor is at its best in the practical-joke stories. These may sometimes be crude, but the humor is almost always rollicking. Perhaps better than any of the other humorous stories they give one a picture of folk life in Egypt.

26

THE DEVIL AND HIS ANGELS[8]

I remember the first deer that I ever saw. My brother and me were out gettin' oat ground ready. I'd never seen any deer. Didn't know what they looked like. In them days we always spoke of the devil and all of his angels.

Well, my brother and me were gettin' oat ground ready. Purty soon a big drove of deer with a big buck at the head came out of the woods. I didn't know what they was. My brother was a big tease. When he saw the deer (he knew that I didn't know what they were), he threw down his ax and said, "My God, there's the devil and all his angels!" And he started to runnin'. It jest about might' near scared me to death. I slammed down my ax and started to runnin', too. My mother heard the noise and she came out and asked what was the matter. I told her what Abraham had said—that was my brother.

The deer moved out through the clearing and purty soon we saw Billy Winchester ride out on a yellow pony. He was a big hunter in that neighborhood. He didn't go very far before we heard his gun.

27

BREAKING UP A DANCE[9]

There was two men named Jim Bridges and Frank Smith that used to run a dry goods store here in Vienny when I first come back from White County. They used to have dances in them days and people would come from miles. They'd dance till purty late.

One time they had a dance two or three miles out of town, and Frank and Jim come in from town. They was a-drinkin', and when they got to the dance they was purty tight.

Frank he had a wooden leg. His leg was cut off a little above the knee.

It was a cold night. The dance was at the house of a widder woman's. The dance got loud. Everybody was havin' a good time, and most of the men was a-drinkin' a little too much. Jim he got to feelin' good, and he thought he'd do something smart. He went out in the yard and caught an old gander. The widder had a lot of geese. He put a ladder up against the chimney and climbed up with the gander. When he got up he dropped the gander down the chimney. The old gander come down the chimney, makin' an awful lot of noise and squallin'. He hit the fire and knocked it in every direction, might' near scarin' people to death. The girls nearly all run out of the house.

Frank then thought he'd do something; so he unstrapped his leg and begin punchin' the boards that was laid up on the cross beams for ceilin', and when the boards begin to fall there wasn't a girl left in the house.

28

THE HAT AND THE MOLASSES[10]

A good many years ago there was a man named Judge Samuel Jackson Robinson Wilson, who lived in our county. The Judge was a dignified man. He always wore a plug hat and a frock coat. The Judge was a relative of mine. Colonel Hay[11] and Judge Wilson were intimate friends. They used to go on sprees together pretty often.

One day Judge Wilson and Colonel Hay went to town to do their trading. They bought a number of things, among which was a jug of molasses. Before they left town they went around to a saloon and got pretty tight. Along in the afternoon they got in the buggy and started home. They were having a hilarious time, paying little attention to their groceries.

I don't know whether you ever noticed it or not, but in one corner of the bed of a buggy there was a little drain-tube. It drained the water out of the buggy-bed.

Well, the jug of molasses got turned over, and about half of it poured into the bed before the Colonel and the Judge discovered the fact. But since the bed was pretty level and the tube fairly small, most of the molasses was still in the buggy. They stopped the horse and began trying to decide what to do. They couldn't afford to lose the molasses.

Finally, Colonel Hay said, "I'll tell you what to do, Sam. You hold your hat under the drain and I'll tilt the buggy, and you can catch all that's been spilled."

"That's a good idea," said Judge Wilson. They got out of the buggy. Judge Wilson got down on his knees and held his hat under the drain, and Colonel Hay tilted a corner of the buggy. After a while they had caught practically all the molasses that had been spilled.

The next problem was what were they going to do with it. They couldn't pour it back into the jug. They decided that the Judge would have to hold it in his hat. But they had to get back into the buggy, and in his condition the Judge wasn't capable of holding his hat full of molasses and climbing into the buggy at the same time.

Colonel Hay came to the rescue again. "I'll get in, Sam, and you hand me the hat, and I'll hold it while you climb in."

Colonel Hay got in the buggy and the Judge handed him the hat. Then the Judge got hold of the dashboard and began to climb into the buggy. Just as he had his foot on the stirrup, Colonel Hay clapped the hat on the Judge's head.

29

THE FLIGHT OF THE NAKED TEAMSTERS[12]

Elizabethtown used to be a prosperous town. There was plenty of labor for every one. You didn't see many idle men on the streets like you do today. We used to have a couple of furnaces here. Both of them were about four or five miles back in the country. The iron was hauled here in wagons and loaded on barges. The teamsters as a rule were pretty tough men.

There was a saloon down on the street that ran along the river. That isn't a street any more. We didn't call them saloons in them days. We called them "doggers." If you'd seen one you'd have known why.

Some young fellers named Grandstalf hauled iron from the furnace to the river. One day they brought loads of iron to town and unloaded it. When they had finished they all went to the "dogger" and got a little something to drink. After they had all they wanted they stripped stark naked and run down and jumped into the river.

Well, they swam around for some time. Finally, one

of the boys got ready to leave, but the others wouldn't come out of the water. They were having too good a time. This one came out and run up to the "dogger" and dressed. He decided that he would pull a joke off on the rest; so he bundled up their clothes and put them on his wagon and drove off home.

After a while the other boys got enough and came out. But when they got up to the saloon, they found that they didn't have no clothes. Well, they got in their wagons without a thread on them and drove naked right down the main street, yelling and whipping their horses.

30

WHOSE 'COON?[13]

I had a powerful 'coon dog—best one I ever had. One morning early I took him 'coon hunting. He treed a 'coon later in a tree on another fellow's land. This other fellow heard the dog barking, and he came down to see what was happening. He said it belonged to him, for it was on his land, and I said it belonged to me because my dog had treed him. We argued around a bit and I says, "I'll tell you what we'll do. We'll compromise. You take the hide and I'll take the meat." Hide wasn't worth much then and I wanted the meat to cook for my dog. "We'll both run home and get axes and cut the tree down," I says.

He started to running hard as he could. He thought I might beat him back and get the 'coon. When he was out of hearing I knocked the 'coon out of the tree with a rock, I put it under my arm and started running as hard as I could. I hid the 'coon, got my ax and beat him back. When I got to the tree I tore up the ground all around. Directly, he came panting up.

"Dog-gone," I says, "that 'coon come down out of

the tree and he and the dog had the awfulest fight I ever saw. You ought to have been here. And that damned 'coon got away."

So I got the hide and the meat, too.

31

BIG JOHN'S PRAYER[14]

Well, I went over to Caseyville one day to buy groceries, and while I was there I bought a jug of whisky. When I got back home my wife says, "There's a note on the table from Bill Hall." Bill used to be our county judge. He was an infidel. He didn't believe in God or Heaven or Hell. Bill wrote me to come over to Battery Rock on the Saline River where two Kentuckians were waiting to play some poker. Bill said we'd skin them out of their hides.

I thought that I'd better take a quart of whisky along, for I was afraid I might get dry before we got through skinning them Kentuckians. But before I got to Battery Rock I decided I'd better hide that whisky because like as not the boys'd drink it all up right off, and I wouldn't have none when I got dry and needed it. So I hid the quart under a log at the side of the road and went on down.

We played poker with them Kentuckians two days and two nights, and I had a hard chill the second night. On the morning of the third day Bill and I was broke. Bill lost twenty dollars and I lost fifteen.

After them Kentuckians left Bill said, "John, we'll have to go to your house for breakfast. I promised Emmy I wouldn't gamble no more, and if I come in at this time a day she'll know I broke my promise."

I said, "All right, Bill, we'll just go to my house." And we started to my house. But as we was a-goin' up the hill, Bill said, "I've about gone as far as I can,

John, I'm so tired. I'd give five dollars for a good drink of whisky." I knowed I had him then.

We walked on up the hill to the log where I hid my quart. I dropped down on the log and said, "I can't go another step, Bill. If you believed in prayer, I'd get down on my knees and ask the Lord to send us something to drink."

"John, are you crazy?" Bill said.

I got down on my knees, but first I looked under the log to see if the quart was still there. It was and I begin to pray:

"O Master, the protector of the weak and the stay of the widows and orphans, Thou hast said in Thy Holy Writ that when two or three are gathered together worshipfully in Thy name that Thou wilt be in their midst. Thou hast promised that whosoever knocketh at the door it shall be opened to him, and whosoever seeketh he shall find. Let Thy abounding mercy rest on us, O Lord, and send us something to quench our thirst. This we ask in the name of Thy crucified son. Amen."

Then I reached under the log and pulled out the quart. "Here it is!" I said.

"Jesus of Nazareth, King of the Jews! Is it whisky, John?"

Bill took the bottle and took a good snort or two. He cleared his throat and handed the bottle to me. "John," he said, "we'll take breakfast at my house. I'm not afraid of airy woman that ever lived."

32

THE MESSAGE TO AUNT MARY[15]

Old Uncle Ike Harris and Uncle George Merritt were two old deer-hunters who lived in our country, and I suppose they were pretty hard bats. There was a widow everyone called Aunt Mary, who lived in the same neighborhood. Aunt Mary had a son named John, who was among the unredeemed. That was a sore trial to her, and she agonized over John's lost condition in prayer and argued and plead with him almost daily, but to no purpose. John turned a deaf ear to all things religious, not even being moved by his poor old mother's tears.

They had no regular preachers in those days, but itinerant preachers used to come around and hold camp meetings and get the whole country worked up to such a point that it took a good many days for people to drop back to normal again. Aunt Mary always took a keen interest in these meetings. She went every night, rain or shine, and she testified every time testimony was called for, always ending with a request that her son John be prayed for. But John was a recalcitrant youth and couldn't be brought under conviction—that was the term applied to a state of penitence.

At last Aunt Mary died, and John was still among the unregenerate.

But finally John was converted. Uncle Ike and Uncle George sat on a log in the woods talking about John's conversion. They wondered why it had taken the Lord so long to answer all the prayers that had been offered up in his behalf. They agreed that it was too bad that Aunt Mary hadn't lived to see John among the redeemed. They wondered if she had heard about it, and how she had felt if she had. However, they didn't want Aunt Mary to fail to hear of John's conversion. Accordingly, they agreed that the first one who should die would take a message to Aunt Mary, telling her of John's conversion.

Pneumonia was the scourge of the pioneers. It killed them like rot kills sheep. There wasn't much in those days that could be done. Medical science hadn't yet learned how to handle the disease.

Well, Uncle George came down with pneumonia. He was in a bad condition and it looked as though he were going to die. In accordance with the agreement, Uncle Ike wrote out a message to Aunt Mary and brought it over to Uncle George.

Uncle Ike said, "George, you remember our agreement about Aunt Mary. It looks like your time has come, and I've brought over a message for you to take to her."

Uncle George moaned from his bed of pain, "Ike, this is no time for frivolity. We've lived a hard life."

"But, George," insisted Uncle Ike, "remember our agreement. We've got to let Aunt Mary know."

"No, no, Isaac! This is no time for frivolity; this is no time for frivolity." And Uncle George refused to take the message.

Uncle George didn't die. He passed the crisis of his illness and began to grow better, and in a few days he was well again.

About a month later Uncle Ike exposed himself and took down with pneumonia. It looked pretty much as though he would die. In the meantime Uncle George had got well. When he heard that Uncle Ike wasn't expected to live, he got the message Uncle Ike had written out and left at his cabin and went over to Uncle Ike's cabin. When he got there he found Uncle Ike in an awful bad shape. He couldn't even talk.

"Ike," said Uncle George, "We decided to let Aunt Mary know about John. I got well, but it looks like you ain't going to pull through. So I brought this message over for you to take to her."

Poor old Uncle Ike was so sick he couldn't even talk, but he motioned Uncle George to put the message in the hunting shirt he (Uncle Ike) was wearing.

33

THE BALL OF FIRE[16]

Ike Edwards wanted a job that another man in the neighborhood had. This man was a stranger, and Ike thought that he would scare him away. He hid inside the paling fence of the graveyard, and when the stranger came riding by Ike said:

"Remember, man, as you are now,
    So once was I;
As I am now you soon will be.
Prepare for death and follow me."

This scared the man and he began to run his horse.

Just then Ike looked up and saw a ball of fire rolling down toward him. He started to running. The fire rolled right down where he was and broke on a stone. Ike ran so fast that he caught up with the horse, and the stranger thought he was a ghost. Ike ran home and fell exhausted in the door. The family had to work with him to bring him to.

34

THE HAUNTED HOUSE OF CENTER[17]

This same Sam Oxford told of a haunted house near Center.[18] It was an old log house and it was called the Old Haunted House. The story he told was a little bit peculiar.

Ever so many people moved to that log house but left after a month or so. They just wouldn't stay there. After night when the lights were blown out, there was a noise that sounded like pebbles being dropped on the floor. Some sounded like small pebbles and some sounded like large ones. The next morning they couldn't find any trace of pebbles. That drove a family away in a short time. Finally, a family moved there that made such a bogerboo about it that it set the whole community to talking. The family left the house as soon as they could find a place to move to.

One night after the family had left the haunted house, there was to be a social at a certain home, but it failed for lack of a fiddler. They all got to talking and discussing the haunted house. One fellow proposed that they all go up there and listen for the pebbles. They took lanterns and went over. They agreed that every fellow would be quiet. All of them stood around the room with their backs to the wall. The fellow who had been arranging the affair said, "Fellows, stand quiet when I blow this lantern out. You won't have to stand long." He blew out the light and they stood there for about two minutes.

There was a fellow standing next to Oxford named Ahab Gullet. He was pretty much of a joker. He nudged Oxford. Oxford put his hand against the wall, and he picked up a piece of chinking and put it in Gullet's hand. Gullet took the hint and shot the chinking against the loft. It broke and fell on the floor in a lot of pieces. That broke up the party. One fellow said, "What did I tell you?" They lit the lantern and got outside.

One man said, "It was just like them people said it was."

Sam and Uncle Ahab never told any of the fellows about the joke, but Sam said they used to have a good laugh to themselves about it.

NOTES ON CHAPTER III

1. Told by Mr. Thomas H. Creighton, Fairfield, Illinois. Mr. Creighton is a lawyer with a practice that has taken him over a large part of the eastern half of Egypt. Being a lover of folk-tales, he has accumulated a large number of stories. This one deals with a couple of local "characters" of Wayne County. This story is not so well known in the county, for memory of Squire Burgh and Col. Hay is fast fading.

2. Told by Mr. Thomas H. Creighton, Fairfield, Illinois. This is only one of the many stories current in Fairfield about Dr. Boggs, who came to Illinois from Kentucky as a result of some trouble in which he was involved. Almost any one in Fairfield can tell some story or anecdote of him.

3. Told by Mr. John M. Harper, Ozark, Illinois. Mr. Harper's stories are well known at Ozark and Vienna, the county-seat of Johnson County. It was his delight to entertain the loafers at the court-house and the county officials with them.

4. This story was also told by John M. Harper, of Ozark. See Note 3, above.

5. Miss Esther Knefelkamp of Belleville, Illinois, gave me this story which she had taken from the dictation of Mr. Henry Juenger, Jr., of Belleville. This is the same story told in Chapter II of the *Original Travels of Baron Munchausen*, but the protagonist is different, and the setting unidentified.

6. This story was told by Lionel C. Smith, Carterville, Illinois. Mr. Smith is a rural mail-carrier in that section in which Cottage Home is situated and has picked up a number of stories. This one is well known in Carterville and the Cottage Home neighborhood.

7. Told by Mr. Wendell Margrave, Carbondale. The story is one that Mr. Margrave learned from his father, whose home was at Thebes, Illinois. It is a well-known story in that neighborhood.

8. Mr. Eliphas E. Hiller, Carbondale, was the narrator of this story, which is known only in his family.

9. Told by Mr. John M. Harper, Ozark, Illinois. See Note 3, page 56. The story is fairly well known in Vienna.

10. This story was secured from Mr. Thomas H. Creighton, Fairfield, Illinois. See Note 1, above.

11. Colonel Hay is the Colonel Lawrence Hay of Story Number 19.

12. Secured from Mr. James Ferrill, Elizabethtown, Illinois, where the story is well known to the older inhabitants.

13. This story and the one that follows were told by the late John Gentry of Cave-in-Rock, Illinois. His stories are personal narratives, but he told them so often that they are pretty generally known in Hardin County. Gentry, who was usually called Big John, had the reputation of being a wag, a reputation that was well deserved. He was the ringleader in most of the pranks played in his neighborhood. Hale and hearty in his old days, he would step nimbly through the patterns of the square dances still fairly common in Hardin County.

14. Told by the late John Gentry, Cave-in-Rock. See Note 13, above.

15. Told by Mr. Thomas H. Creighton, Fairfield. Apparently the story is not widely known.

16. Told by Mr. Gordon Lowry, Shawneetown. Mr. Lowry formerly lived in Hardin County, the scene of this story, which is generally known in the neighborhood in which the event happened. Typical of the stories from that county, it has a ghostly tone.

17. Related by Mr. E. N. Hall, Elizabethtown.

18. The Sam Oxford of this story is the one who is mentioned in "The Rock Creek Ghost," No. 47, pp. 78–80.

CHAPTER IV

GRAVEYARD STORIES

Graveyards rival in popularity haunted houses as settings for stories of a ghostly character. Tales which I have called graveyard stories are not properly ghost-stories but are grisly narratives with scenes laid in cemeteries. Usually, they are concerned with such incidents as burial of living persons, grave-robberies, and deaths from fright. Graveyard stories seem to be more popular among people of German descent than among the descendants of other nationalities; five of the seven stories included in this chapter were told by people of German ancestry.

35

BURIED ALIVE[1]

Before the time that embalming of the dead was practised, many people were pronounced dead, only to come alive again. This story has to do with a middle-aged woman who had been ill for two weeks and then died. After a wake had been held, as was the custom, she was buried.

It happened the night of the day of her burial that a group of grave-robbers visited the cemetery and noticed the new grave and decided to rob it. The chief object of these robbers was not to steal the bodies, but rather any jewelry that might have been buried with them.

When the lid of the coffin was raised, they were glad to see a ruby ring as well as a plain gold ring on the victim's second finger of the left hand. They were disappointed when they found that it was impossible to remove the rings over the first joint. At last, as they hated to leave these two valuable rings, they decided to cut the finger.

As the knife pierced the flesh, the robbers were startled by a slight movement of the hand. At about the same time the corpse sat up in the coffin—and the robbers took to their heels.

The woman climbed out of her coffin and went home, where she explained that she had been conscious of the fact that she had been pronounced dead but was unable to move or speak to prevent being buried.

36

DEATH OF A GRAVE-ROBBER[2]

In the early days when it was necessary for the medical students to acquire bodies in whatever manner they could, a student was digging into a freshly-made grave. As he raised the lid of the coffin and held the lantern to see the corpse, he was confronted by a woman stark mad.

The next day the woman and the student were found in the grave dead. It was apparent that a fierce struggle had taken place, and the strength of the mad woman was more than that of the student, as she was still clutching the student's throat.

The community then realized that the woman had been buried alive and had gone stark mad when she learned the truth.

37

THE DEAD HANGMAN[3]

Did ye ever hear the story about a dead man hangin'
a live one? Yeh, a dead man hung a live one! One time
there was a saloon-keeper that lived here.[4] He was a
great big fat man—one of the biggest men in this whole
country. There was a young doctor here in town that
hadn't been out of school long. This doctor used to joke
the saloon-keeper about buying his body. The doctor
said, "How much will you take for your body after
you're dead?"

The saloon-keeper he said, "Five dollars." And the
doctor give the saloon-keeper five dollars, and they drew
up a contract that the doctor was to have the saloon-
keeper's body when he was dead.

It wasn't long before the saloon-keeper died and
they buried him. It took an awful big coffin for him and
a big grave. They went ahead and buried him, but the
doctor had bought his body and he aimed to have it.
So one night he had a man named Smith to dig it up.
Smith went there to the cemetery and dug up the body,
but he couldn't get it out of the grave, it was so heavy.
Well, he went and hooked up a team and got a chain and
came back to pull the body out.

Smith he put the chain around the body and run it
across a purty high fence so the team would pull the
body upward. Then he went and hitched the team to
the other end of the chain across the fence. Then Smith
started the horses. Well, the chain came loose and got
wrapped around Smith's neck. The old saloon-keeper
was heavier than Smith; so his body just slipped back
into the grave and pulled Smith up on the fence and
hung him.

The next mornin' early some man was a-walkin' along
near the cemetery, and he saw Smith a-hangin' there.
He went on the inside of the fence, and he saw the

saloon-keeper at the other end of the chain. Then he run down town and spread the alarm about a dead man a-hangin' a live one. Everybody got excited and run to the cemetery, and they took Smith down. And people said that's what he got for robbin' a grave.

*　　*　　*

The next four tales are variants of one story: two of them were found in Belleville, which is in the northwestern part of Egypt; one of them in Carterville, a town in the coal-fields near the central part of the section; and the last one in Elizabethtown, which is in the southeastern part of Southern Illinois, on the Ohio River. This story seems to have a wider currency than any other which I have found, and it is difficult to see why.

38

A

THE GIRL WHO DIED OF FRIGHT[5]

One time there was a girl who said she didn't believe in haints.* She said she wouldn't be afraid to go to a graveyard at night by herself. They told her she'd better not, but she claimed she wasn't afraid. Some one dared her to go. One evening about dark she started.

As the girl got close to the graveyard, she began to have a creepy feelin'. By the time she got to the cemetery she was about scared to death, but she went on in. She decided that she'd stick a stick in a grave to prove to them that she'd been to the graveyard.

She hunted around and found a stick and went up to a grave for to put it in as proof. But when she went to job† it in the ground, she got her apron underneath

* I. e., "haunts" ghosts.
† Job=jab.

the point of the stick. It jerked her down, and she thought a ghost had reached up out of the grave and was pullin' her in. It scared her so bad that she just dropped over dead right there.

Next morning her folks got uneasy about her not comin' home, and they got out to lookin' for her, and they found her lyin' across a grave with her apron pinned under a stick that she'd stuck in the ground.

I guess maybe the sudden scare caused her to have heart-failure. Anyhow she was scared of ghosts.

B

THE LOST BET[6]

A group of men were gathered at a saloon one evening. Among the men was a man who was always bragging about his bravery. This group of men decided to see how brave he really was. They bet him fifty dollars that he was not brave enough to go to a certain grave in the town churchyard at midnight and drive a stake two feet into the grave of this man. The man said that he would accept the wager.

On a given night at midnight this party started for the graveyard. The party was to wait at the gate for this man, while he went in to drive the stake into the grave. The ground around this particular grave was supposed to be haunted.

The man was dressed in the fashion of the day. He wore a long linen coat called an ulster. He was very frightened and in a very great hurry. In his haste he unknowingly drove the tail of his coat into the grave with the stake. When he thought that he had completed his brave task, he started to leave very hastily. Thinking that his coat had been caught by a ghost and that he would be drawn into the grave himself, he died of fright.

After waiting for some time, the party went into the graveyard in search of him. They found him lifeless, lying across the haunted grave. He had not only lost his bet but also his life in his attempt to prove his bravery.

C

THE WOMAN WHO DIED OF FRIGHT[7]

A party was being held. In the course of the evening the conversation drifted to ghosts and cemeteries. Several of the guests honestly confessed their fear of cemeteries after dark, which caused them to become the subject of much teasing. One lady in particular kidded and chided so very much that one of the tormented decided to call her bluff. At the close of the party he dared her to go to the cemetery and take with her a stick which was to be driven into a designated grave.

The next morning the caretaker found the woman dead. In kneeling to hammer the stick into the grave she had driven it through her dress. She had evidently died from fright when she found herself fast after having completed her task.

D

THE MAN WHO DIED OF FRIGHT[8]

Bravery was the subject of the discussion when Frank Morris arrived at the Hillocks' party. Frank had been taken in as a good fellow when he came to Jamesburg six years before.

Jamesburg was an old town with many traditions and superstitions.

At the time Frank arrived the discussion had been very quiet, but as Frank took to arguing the discussion became more heated. Many of the men present were citing incidents which they thought were unquestionably the bravest they had ever seen or heard.

One fellow was telling of a farmer in a town close by who drove through the cemetery in order to get to town early. It seemed that the natives were impressed with this, but not so Frank. Surprised at Frank's attitude, one of the men made a wager that Frank wouldn't do the same. Not being afraid, Frank accepted, and it was decided that he was to take a hammer with him and when he came to the freshly dug grave he was to lower himself into it and hammer the nail into the pine box in the grave. To be sure that this was accomplished the party was to gather at dawn at the open grave to see if Frank had carried out his boast.

When the party arrived at the grave the next morning, they were shocked to see Frank lying face down in the box. Upon investigating they found he was dead and the tail of his coat was nailed to the box.

NOTES ON CHAPTER IV

1. Miss Irene Mache, Belleville, told this tale, which she had obtained from a Mrs. Shrimp, also of Belleville. Belleville is an industrial city near St. Louis with a large German population. Inhabitants of that city have preserved folk-tales and ballads to a degree that is surprising when one considers all of the resources of entertainment at their disposal.

2. This story was also told by Miss Irene Mache. She learned it from Mrs. Katherine Brauer of St. Louis, Missouri.

3. The late Frank Schumaker, Grand Tower, Illinois, told me this story in the summer of 1928. The incident was supposed to have happened in Grand Tower many years ago. Today perhaps not many people in that town remember this story; at least, none of the other inhabitants mentioned it to me. Mr. Schumaker said that it had been so long since he had told any of the stories that he knew that he had forgotten most of them.

4. Grand Tower, Illinois.

5. Mrs. Mary U. Stallion, Elizabethtown, related this version of the story to me in the summer of 1928. A good many people there must have heard her tell this particular tale, for she had a reputation in the town as a story-teller.

6. This variant was given to me by Miss Maxine Moore, Carterville. She learned it from her parents. Apparently, the story is not widely known in that town. Tales of the mines, usually of a practical-joke nature, are popular there.

7. Variant C came from Miss Irene Mache, Belleville, who obtained it from Mrs. Henrietta Knefelkamp, of Belleville. The fact that two variants of the tale came from that city seems to indicate that it is fairly well known.

8. Miss Irene Mache, Belleville, also supplied Variant D. This variant she learned from Dr. William A. Kneedler, of Belleville.

CHAPTER V

GHOST-STORIES

GHOST-STORIES have a wide currency in Egypt. They are perhaps more frequently told than any other kind of folk-tales. For most Egyptians they have been the terror and the delight of childhood and are likely to be the chief stock-in-trade of story-tellers. One narrator, recalling her own experience, observed that the children "sat spitless as if turned to stone," while they listened to ghost stories that were told at neighborhood gatherings. These tales are most popular in the rural communities of the Ozark Foothills, but one finds them also in a highly industrialized city like Belleville.

One is inclined to associate the ghost-story with an ancient dame in a chimney-corner, but men tell them more often than women. Approximately two-thirds of the tales in this collection were related by men. Nor can one say that the narrator is an unlettered farmer; very often he is, but the best teller of ghost-stories I met was a college-bred man who was at the time serving as county superintendent of schools in Hardin County. In most cases the narrator takes pains to disclaim belief in the ghosts that he delights in telling about, but now and then the collector finds one who is inclined to be credulous, though he may hesitate to admit the fact.

The apparitions in these ghost-tales appear in various guises, sometimes as a man of natural or heroic size, sometimes as a woman, in one instance as a hand. Frequently, they take the form of an animal—a dog, with or without a head, or a cat. More often they assume the form of an inanimate object: a laundry-bag, a bolster, a carpet-bag, a coffin, or a light. In one tale, the apparition appears as a rumbling wagon drawn by a team of horses and driven by a man. Most frequently, however, it makes its presence known by sound. Perhaps the most common sound is footsteps; occasionally, it speaks or screams and meows like a cat. In one story, the apparition pounds on a barrel or makes a noise that resembles the sound of a rolling barrel. In another story, it taps on all of the windows of the house. Sometimes it makes its presence known by the rattling or the dragging of a chain on the floor, or it may reveal itself by a noise that resembles the scratching of chickens upon a floor. One ghost causes a clock, which had long stood silent, to strike; another stirs the fire; and still another sets an invisible milk-pail on the floor. Some ghosts seem to have only one sound at their command; others appear to be masters of a whole array of sound-effects.

In about half of these stories the ghost has no motive for appearing, unless it is prompted by an impulse to mischief; in the rest it has a clearly defined purpose. Several of these ghosts play benevolent rôles; in three stories they lead people to treasure-troves; in two they warn of impending danger. A number of them presage death to a friend or relative or give notice that death has occurred.

Supernatural visitations in which the apparition appears to give notice of impending danger or death are usually spoken of as warnings or "tokens." Warnings do not always give rise to stories; now and then one hears only the bald statement that a certain person once received such a visitation. "Three nights before the brother of my mother died," one woman said, "a little wagon travelled around the house and over the wooden walk."[1] A daughter of the narrator mentioned in the last sentence observed: "I was sitting in the house reading. Someone came into the hall and set a milk-bucket down. I went all over the house, thinking that it might be Grandmother. I went up to the attic. Then I went out to the barn, where I found Grandmother milking.'"[2] These bald statements are disappointing, for they are but the skeletons upon which ghost-stories are built. With a little more imagination on the part of some teller, one would get a fair tale. A person with a rich imagination would be sure to see a causal relationship between the sound of the milk-pail and some later misfortune. Equally unsatisfactory is this account of the "Dutton Ghost": "Edward Penell said that when Will Dutton's wife lay a corpse, a light began going around the room. It got higher and higher. Everyone in the room saw it, but no one said a thing."[3]

The ghosts in the first ten stories seem to have no purpose in making their presence known, unless it is to frighten people. These stories are told for the sake of the ghosts.

*　　*　　*

39

THE BUNDLE AT HOLLOWAY HILL[4]

My uncle lived near a hill called Holloway Hill.[5] This was a big hill with a woods on top. The main road passed this hill and several people had seen a big white bundle (the kind you see the laundryman carry from houses these days) come out of the woods on this hill and tumble down the hill to the road. But, strange to say, no one had ever seen the bundle go up the hill. Well, if a farmer were driving an open wagon the bundle would jump on top of the wagon behind him. Sometimes the bundle jumped to the back of a buggy, but more often the bundle jumped to the back of the horse until the farmer got to the top of the hill; then it disappeared. This story got around in the neighborhood, and people said that Holloway Hill was haunted. Now, there was a mail-carrier named Charlie Thompson who laughed at this story and said if he ever met the bundle he'd speak to it.

One evening as he was driving home his buggy broke down at the foot of the hill. He aimed to fix it, but night came on and he had no lantern. He walked to my uncle's house to get a lantern. My uncle came with him and helped fix the buggy. He offered Charlie the lantern and Charlie told uncle he'd return it the next morning. Uncle started home; Charlie started up the hill, and here came the bundle and stopped alongside Charlie's buggy. Charlie yelled, "Who are you?" The bundle said nothing. Charlie yelled a few cuss-words at the bundle. Up jumped the bundle and banged Charlie on the back of the head. Charlie let out a blood-curdling scream. My uncle came running. The bundle was gone.

40

THE WEIDERHOLD GHOST[6]

My uncle, J. J. Lowry, ran a customs thrashing-machine. My father, J. M. Lowry, fired the engine, and John Lane fed the thrashing-machine. One year they thrashed wheat at the Weiderhold Farm about a mile down the road. In the evening after supper, the three men were upstairs in a bedroom with John Hughes. John Lane was already in bed and asleep. But my father and uncle and Hughes were still up, looking at some books.

Suddenly, there was a tapping at the window. It ran all around the house, tapping on the windows, coming back to the window of the room where they all were. It scared the three men who were up, and they asked the ghost what it wanted, but it wouldn't answer. Finally, they woke Lane and told him to ask it what it wanted. Lane said, "You'd better come to bed and let that thing alone." But when the tapping continued on the window, he said, "What do you want in the name of the Lord?"

Then there was the awfulest clatter and screaming outside, and the noise stopped. They all went to bed at once.

My father never believed in ghosts. He was a preacher, and he always said that nobody would come back to earth after death. For if a body went to heaven, he wouldn't want to come back; and if he went to hell, he couldn't. But that ghost changed his belief.

41
THE BARREL GHOST[7]

This story was told by a man named Oxford, who was present one night when the ghost appeared. There was an old man who lived in Hardin County across the Saline Creek. He had two sick children. Something kept bothering them all night long. They told the neighbors, and the neighbors came in to stay with them. The neighbors talked a lot about it, and one night they gathered to find out what the walking was.

The family lived in an old store building. There was a long room with three rooms built on the side. That night they heard some one walking in the north room. It walked through all the rooms and went out to an old log house, which was used as a smoke house, and began to pound. It sounded like pounding on a barrel. The woman said, "There it goes." No one would go out to see what it was. The woman offered to go out and carry a light if the men would go with her, but no one would go.

Suddenly, something started out of the shed on the side of the log house, like a barrel rolling. They didn't investigate, and they never found out what it was.

42

THE WOMAN IN THE BLACK BONNET[8]

A distant cousin of mine, a Mrs. Craig, once lived in that same house (the house mentioned in the story above). As she went into the kitchen each morning, a woman in black would go out. She wore a long dress. Mrs. Craig never saw the woman's face, for her back was always turned.

43

THE GHOSTLY HAND[9]

My grandparents lived in a log cabin but later on built a nice two-story frame house across the road. They kept the log house as a place to store things. Well, times weren't so good; so they decided to rent the log house. But people wouldn't stay in that house, for ghosts walked there. Once late at night my grandparents were awakened by the creaking of the big barn gate. They looked out and saw a team with no driver pass through the gate and go to the log house and then disappear. Next morning the gate was still open. That night some of the tenants heard a noise like the falling and clattering of every dish and pan in the house. The next night when the hired man went to put corn in the feed-box another ghostly hand took out an ear of corn. Since that time ghosts walk around the old log house.

44

HETHERINGTON'S GHOST[10]

On the Ford Road there was a fellow who lived in a nice two-story house near Enterprise School. His name was John Hetherington, and he dealt in cattle and hogs. He was a pretty prosperous man.

One night he was passing along in front of Enterprise School house, which is about one-fourth to one-half a mile from his home. He was driving two horses that pulled the buggy at a trot. Suddenly, a man ran down from the school-yard toward the buggy. The horses were in a trot, but the man ran down easily to the buggy. Hetherington spoke to him, but he didn't answer. Hetherington whipped his horses into a run, and the man trotted along, easily keeping up with the buggy.

When Hetherington drove up to the lot gate, he found it was open. I don't know what he would have done if it hadn't been. I suppose he would have run the team right into the gate. He looked at the post to keep from smashing his buggy as he was making the drive through the gate. When he looked back to see the man, he was gone.

The next day Hetherington went to a doctor, who told him that he was working too hard and that he had had an hallucination. However, Hetherington sold his farm as soon as he could find a buyer and left there. He went to Harrisburg.

45

THE DUG HILL BOGER[11]

Frank Corzine seed a boger one night as he was a-comin' through Dug Hill on horseback. It was sometime between sundown and dark. Suddenly, as Frank was a-ridin' along, the figure of a man appeared. The figure was between nine and eleven foot tall. It wore black pants, a light shirt, and had a scarf hangin' over its shoulders with both ends dangling in front. When Frank first seed it, the thing was about thirty yards or more behind him a-walkin', but within the twinklin' of of an eye it was up within four or five feet of Frank, and it walked all the way through the hill with him.

Frank was might' near scared to death, and his horse got scared, too, and lunged and jumped and broke a strap on the saddle and started to runnin'. The horse ran with Frank on him for about three hundred yards to the house of Dr. Russell. Frank was goin' for the doctor for a cholera case. His wife was sick with the cholera.

When Dr. Russell come out of his house, he seed that Frank was scared and the horse was scared, too. Frank was pale and couldn't talk much, and the horse was standin' there, snortin' and tremblin' all over just like horses do when they git a bad scare. Dr. Russell accused Frank of bein' scared. The doctor told Frank he knowed he'd seed something while he was a-comin' through Dug Hill. The doctor said that you could tell that the horse had seed something that had scared it mighty bad by the way he was a-standin' there snortin' and tremblin' all over. Frank couldn't say much at first, and Dr. Russell says again, "You know you seed something, Frank." Then Corzine says, "Yes, I seed a man between nine and eleven foot tall. He caught up with me and come all the way through Dug Hill with me." And Dr. Russell says, "The rascal walked through Dug Hill with me a few nights ago." And the doctor goes ahead and describes the same man Corzine seen when he was a-comin' through Dug Hill. It wore black pants, a white shirt, and had a scarf hangin' over its shoulders and danglin' in front just like the boger Frank seed.

Dr. Russell said he wouldn't come to see Corzine's wife that night. He was scared of the boger. And the doctor didn't come till the next mornin' after daylight. He waked up eight men, though, and had them git shot-guns and go through Dug Hill with Frank. But the boger didn't show itself to them when they went through the hill.

46

THE HEADLESS DOG[12]

One night a good many years ago Uncle Nig Hobbs went to town to get something. He had to pass along Ford's Ferry Road right by Potts's Hill. They say that that road and Potts's Hill are haunted. People have heard groans and dull blows that sound like someone was being knocked in the head. And some folks claim that they've seen things along there.

Nig had been to mill, and he had a sack of meal on his back.

When Nig got near Potts's Hill, he saw a big dog without any head. It scared him nearly to death, and he started to running. He dropped his meal and bursted the sack, but he didn't know it. He ran up the hill to Uncle Marsh Ledbetter's. Uncle Marsh laughed and haw-hawed and cursed at Nig's story. He got a lantern and went back with Uncle Nig to get his meal, but they didn't find the meal.

Uncle Marsh argued that Uncle Nig had seen a stump. They got out in the field where Nig had seen the headless dog and found some stumps sure enough, but Nig didn't think any one of them was his dog. He claimed that he saw the outline of a dog. He saw four legs distinctly, and the dog had a big white spot on his breast.

47

THE ROCK CREEK GHOST[13]

I expect that it's been reported that at least two hundred people have seen the Rock Creek Ghost, and more than two hundred people have heard it. It has been seen at Rock Creek Church. One mile south of the Rock Creek store the road crosses a small branch. It is near this crossing that the ghost was seen and heard.

A fellow by the name of John T. Ledbetter used to be sheriff of this county, and a fellow by the name of John Caghill was deputy. In passing along this road near the branch one night, they claimed that their horse became frightened. It wasn't very dark. I suppose it was a little after dusk. They saw ahead of the horse what seemed to be an old-fashioned carpet-bag rolling down the road. They were both officers and, of course, they had revolvers. They pulled out their guns and both of them shot twice apiece. When the smoke cleared away, there was nothing to be seen. They went on home and the ghost didn't appear again.

The Rock Creek Ghost has been seen in that form, but more often it has been seen in the form of a dog.

One night Sam Oxford was coming from church with a bunch of boys. Sam was talking and laughing. He was always a great hand for fun. As they were walking along near this branch, a big shepherd dog came out of the bushes at the side of the road and trotted up to where the men were walking. Sam was a big rough fellow that acted on the spur of the moment. He blazed away with his great big foot and thought he would give the dog a vicious kick that would send it to the other side of the road. But the kick went right on through the dog without coming into contact with anything, and it gave Sam pretty much of a jerk. The dog just kept trotting along at their side and finally disappeared in the bushes on the other side of the road.

That experience had a marked effect on Sam Oxford. It made him think that there was something besides material objects in this world.

A great many people claim that they've seen this dog.

About thirty years ago another fellow named Oxford (he was related to Sam Oxford) had to pass through Rock Creek to see a girl he was courting. The girl's name was Ford. He saw that dog until even his horse got frightened. He finally got to the point that, when he was passing along there, he would shut his eyes and whip his horse and make it run for a quarter of a mile before he would open his eyes again.

The ground has been cleared up for some time on both sides of the road. You don't hear of any one seeing the ghost now, but people still hear things that don't sound very good.

People used to tell of someone following them along the inside of the field along the road. They couldn't see anything, though, because the roadside was all grown up with thicket. Ever so many people have heard sounds like someone walking in the leaves on the other side. I heard that myself. I was with five or six boys one night, coming along the road, and we heard it very distinctly. We were going to church. One of the boys said we'd strike a match and go in and see what it was. About all the fellows had matches but me. One of them proposed that they would hold the match if I would go up and see what it was. I said, "All right." They struck two or three matches, and they went out. Presently, they decided that something was wrong. Finally, one man put two matches together and struck them. They were snuffed out like someone blowing them out. The fellow said, "Boys, where you can't get matches to burn, something's wrong. Come on! Let's get out of here!" He started and we followed.

After I went to college, I came back home and

preached for the Rock Creek Church for three years. I passed there at all times of the day and night, and I heard the phenomenon. One night as I was going along that road, I heard it walking on the other side of the fence distinctly. I rode on a little way and heard it keeping right along with me but a little ahead. My horse was a little frightened. I jumped down and hitched my horse to the fence. (A fence had been built along the road by then.) I went out into the bushes and saw an old cow browsing. I walked back to where I first heard the noise, seventy-five yards back, and found another cow.

Oxford was a man to be relied on. He didn't believe in things of that sort. There is no doubt that things have been seen and heard there that are hard to explain. Ever so many people's horses have pricked up their ears when there was nothing to be seen.

48

THE FLYING WAGON[14]

A feller by the name of Bill Smith told me this story. Bill ain't jest exactly in his right mind; he's a sort o'half idiot, I guess. He's still a-livin' at Jonesboro, and you might see him on the streets. If you'd ask him about it, he'd tell you the same thing I'm a-tellin' you if he'd talk to you.

Bill was a-haulin' off corn one day. It's been a long time ago. He'd hauled off three loads of corn that day and was a-goin' home after dark. He had to pass through Dug Hill fer he lived over in the bottoms. He'd jest about got half-way down the hill, goin' west, when the neck-yoke of one of his horses come off, and Bill had to stop the wagon right there on the grade and git out to fix the yoke.

The ground was froze hard, fer it was in December when he was a-haulin' the corn off. And the wagons that come over the roads done a heap of rattlin' on account of the shape they was in. You could hear the wagon comin' a long way off.

As Bill was down there a-fixin' the yoke, he heared the awfulest racket a man ever did hear. It sounded like some drunk man a-drivin' an empty wagon over the road as fast as the horses could go. Bill thought maybe it was one of his buddies that was a-haulin' off corn with him, comin' home drunk. It scared Bill to death nearly, fer he knew that there wasn't enough room fer the wagon to git by on account of the road bein' so narrow, and Bill knowed he couldn't git out of the way. It looked like him and his horses might git killed. Bill looked back up the hill and hollered as loud as he could, but it didn't do no good. The racket kept gittin' nearer and nearer. Bill didn't know what to do. He knowed that the driver couldn't stop the wagon in time.

The noise was on the brink of the hill. Bill looked up, and he realized a few minutes later that the noise of the wagon was in the air above him and not on the road a-tall.

Bill looked up in the air, and he seed comin' over the crest of the hill a heavy pair of black horses a-pullin' a heavy wagon with side-boards on. A man was a-settin' in the wagon a-drivin'. The horses were a-runnin' up there in the air jest like they was on the ground, and the wheels of the wagon was a-turnin' jest like they was on the ground, and the wagon was makin' a awful lot of racket like a wagon does when it's drove over rough, froze ground. The wagon and team passed right over Bill's head and struck the crest of another hill, and Bill couldn't see it any more, but he heard the noise of the wagon after it had got two miles away.

*   *   *

In the remaining stories of this chapter the apparitions have a purpose in appearing. They are ghosts from an unquiet grave, troubled by worldly cares or moved by resentment at indignities that they have received at the hands of the living or prompted by a spirit of benevolence toward some mortal.

* * *

49

GRANNY BIGSBY'S GHOST[15]

A good many people have seen lights that looked like a big ball of fire floating along. Some people have said that they were mineral lights, but I don't know. One night a young fellow named Hobbs and I went to a place where it had been seen particularly. We had gone to get a couple of girls to take to church. When we got to the house where they stayed, there wasn't a light. The girls were already gone, but we weren't sure. We halloed, but no one answered, and the house was still dark. I told Hobbs they were gone. He said he didn't think so. He thought maybe they had put out all the lights and were watching for us and were quiet in order to play a joke on us. He thought maybe they had decided not to go to church.

The house stood on a knoll with a hollow to the left of the gate that ran about a hundred yards and joined another hollow that came back to the right of the gate.

While we were standing there at the gate quiet and Hobbs was looking eastward, he saw a ball of fire about the size of a washing tub going very fast along the east hollow. I never saw anything like it, and it scared me. Hobbs grabbed me by the arm and said, "Look yonder! Look yonder!"

I said, "What is it?"

"Somebody on a horse with a lantern." But it looked too big for a lantern.

It was a cloudy night, as dark as dark could be.

The light followed that little hollow to the left of the gate and along the little curve to where that hollow joined the one that came back on the right-hand side of the gate. It came up the right hollow and came up the bank where we were. It stopped moving when it was about forty feet from us and twenty-five or thirty feet high and burned. As it burned down smaller and smaller it turned red. When that thing burned out, that was the darkest place I ever saw on this earth.

I got hold of Hobbs and said, "Let's go!"

"Go where?" he asked. "To Church."

"No, let's go home."

"Let's stay and see if it will come again."

I said, "No, I've seen all I want to see."

We stayed there a while, but it didn't appear any more. We decided not to go to Church. We went back to the place where we were working and went to bed. The next morning at the breakfast table we told our experience. Mr. Patten, the man we were working for, leaned back in his chair and laughed. He said it was nothing more than a mineral light blown by the wind.

I remember more or less what I said at the time. "Carried by the wind!" said I. "Thunder and grindstones, there wasn't enough air moving to stir a leaf." And there wasn't any wind that night and hadn't been any all afternoon. I've never been able to explain why that light floated down one hollow and took another one and floated back.

Mrs. Walton always said that it was Granny Bigsby going to see where her money was buried. Granny Bigsby was an old midwife and Indian herb-doctor. Her husband was a counterfeiter. Granny had a lot of money hid out. No one knew where she hid it. Mrs. Walton was a niece of Granny Bigsby's, and she knew where Granny kept her money. She'd seen her go to it many times. Since Granny's death she had seen a light go to it many times. I used to ask her why she didn't go get the money if she knew where it was. She said, "I would if I thought Granny wanted me to have it."

50

THE MISER'S GOLD
A[16]

In the early days of Pope County there were log cabins scattered here and there over the country, the homes usually of pioneer families. People migrating from Kentucky and Tennessee, however, usually had a hard time finding shelter at night, for, as a rule, the early settlers had about as many children as his cabin would hold.

Down in the Gooseneck (which is the name usually given to the southern part of Pope County) there was a deserted log cabin that would have been a blessing to travelers if it hadn't been haunted. A man who had had a lot of money had lived there at one time. The robbers had visited his house one night and killed him. Since then a ghost had haunted the place, and none of the people in the neighborhood would come near it after dark.

One evening a family migrating from Kentucky stopped at the old deserted cabin to spend the night. With wolves and panthers still plentiful enough, most people felt safer behind barred doors. The log cabin offered ample protection; in fact, it was one of the best cabins in the neighborhood, even having a cellar underneath. The children gathered wood and the mother started a fire in the fireplace, while the father took a bucket and went up the road to the next house for water, since the water at the deserted cabin wasn't fit for use.

It was about a mile to the next cabin. When he got there, he was told that the cabin he had stopped at was haunted, or "hainted" as folks said, and that no one could stay there. They told him such awful stories that he was afraid to return. It was beginning to grow dark—which made things look more frightful still. After much debate and hesitation, he decided to spend the night with these people and leave his family to its fate.

His wife, being a devout Christian, got out a candle and lighted it and opened her Bible, which she read every night, and began reading while she waited for her husband to return with the water. But he didn't return.

After a while when it grew dark, she heard someone walking up to the door, but she supposed it was her husband and thought no more of it, until a strange man walked into the room. He walked slowly and deliberately up to her without a word and didn't stop till he was directly in front. Now, the woman was braver than her husband; being a devout Christian, she put her trust in the Lord. She spoke up and said, "What in the name of the Lord do you want?" Old folks say for one to ask a ghost, "What in the name of the Lord do you want?" Then the ghost will tell you and not return again.

The ghost said, "Follow me."

She took up her candle and her Bible and followed the ghost, trusting in the Lord. He led her down a flight of stairs into the cellar and said, pointing toward the northwest corner, "Dig down there and you will find a pot of gold." After saying that he vanished and was never seen again.

The next morning the husband returned and they dug up the pot of gold, and they were well provided for after that.

They claim that the ghost had haunted the house, trying to tell someone about the pot of gold, but no one had been brave enough to listen to it before the woman.

B[17]

This story took place down in Tennessee. There was an old house that was supposed to be haunted. Every one that moved in would live there a day or two and move away. One time a man bought the place and moved there. He was married and had two small children. The first night they stayed there it was cold, and they didn't have any matches. The man was scary, and the matches gave him an excuse to get away. He went to a neighbor's house to borrow some matches and left his wife and two children there alone. He never came back that night.

While he was gone, a man without a head came down the stairs, crying and moaning. This scared the woman, but she would not run away from her babies. The man kept coming toward her. He spoke to her and then began talking. He told her that he had been killed for his money by robbers. He said that he had hated everyone and had wished to live there by himself. He said the robbers didn't find the money. He told her where the money was and that she could have it.

The next day her husband returned, and she told him what had happened during the night. They found the money hidden in the fireplace. They fixed the farm up and lived happily thereafter.

C[18]

There was a haunted house out here in the hills. The reason it was haunted was because an old miser had been killed there. The old miser had lots of money, and one night some men came there and tried to make him tell where he hid it. He wouldn't tell them; so they slashed his throat. Ever since the house has been haunted. People claimed that if you'd go there and stay all night, the old miser would come back and tell where he kept his gold, but nobody was brave enough to spend the night there.

Finally, there was a man who was brave enough to stay there. He went to the house one evening and went to bed. He hadn't been in bed long before he was sound asleep. Along in the night he was awakened by a bump, bump noise. He sat up in bed. The noise continued. It was something coming down the stairs. Whatever it was at last reached the floor and came to the door, opened it, and came into the room. The man was almost scared to death at what he saw. There stood the old miser with his throat slashed and bleeding horribly, with a coffin in his arms. The man was so badly frightened that he couldn't speak.

The ghost said: "You are the only man who is brave enough to stay here all night, and I'll show you where my gold is hid."

The old man took the man to a tree, and he found a rich treasure.

51

THE DUTCHMAN'S GHOST STORY[19]

Joe Kiestler was a German right from the ole country. My ole Uncle Ike—he was an ole bachelor—kept him. He told the Dutchman to come there to live as one of the family. Uncle Ike didn't pay him a regular salary. He gave him money to live on an' hogs an' cattle to git a start on.

Joe was a great lover of cats an' dogs. The Dutchman slept upstairs an' the cats would sleep with him. Finally

Joe got sick an' he was bad off. They had to carry him downstairs. He had an ole silver watch he thought a great deal of, an' he wouldn't consent to go down unless the watch went. They finally got him down an' he died. He requested that the watch be buried with him. They didn't do it.

Well, they had an ole-fashion clock that stood in the hall—a grandfather clock about eight feet high. But the clock hadn't run for twenty-odd years. So one day those cats—the Dutchman had about two dozen of them—they got out in the hall and circled around the clock, an' the clock began to strike, an' the cats began to meow. An' they counted the strokes, an' if it struck onct it struck two hundred an' eighty times.

The nex' thing, they could hear something scratchin' like an ole hen. They looked under the bed an' they never seen anything. An' the nex' thing sounded to them like a noise made by a big log chain bein' drug down the stairway. The cats got bunched again around the ole clock an' begin to meow. An' then my ole uncle, that lived there, he stepped out in the hall with the cats meowin' an' the clock strikin', an' he says, "Joe, what is it you want? If they's anything you want say so." He talked to him like he was a live man. Right then the cats stopped, an' the clock stopped, an' it never struck any more.

*   *   *

In the next two tales the ghosts return to protest against the misdeeds of erring mates. The ghost in the first one brings about the death of the husband; in the second, it merely frightens the wife and her second husband for their unthrifty ways. The wife's ghost appears in the form of a woman; the husband's in the form of a jumping-jack about a foot high.

52

THE DUTTON HILL GHOST[20]

There was a young man and his wife who lived near Dutton Hill in Hardin County. The wife was a lovely woman, and she had a beautiful black horse. The man was a two-timer; he was slipping over across the grave-yard to see another woman. When the wife found it out, she grieved herself to death. On her death-bed she begged him to take care of her horse. She was buried in the cemetery that he went across.

After her death, he rode the horse across the cemetery to see the woman. And as he crossed, his wife's ghost would come out of the grave and get on behind him. He would dig his spurs into the flanks of the horse, trying to get away from the ghost. But it would stay with him till he was past the cemetery.

He didn't take care of the horse at all but mistreated it and kept its sides sore with the spur. One night as he was racing through the cemetery, trying to escape his wife's ghost, the horse fell and threw him against a tombstone and killed him.

53

THE ERNSHAW GHOST[21]

The Ernshaw House was haunted. Ernshaw had died and his wife had married again. She and her second husband was running through all that he had left. He came back, and it scared his wife and her second husband. A man named McDowell stayed all night once to find out about the ghost. The ghost appeared in his room and pulled the quilts off his bed. He pulled one of them over him and said, "Be fair. Leave me one of the quilts." But the ghost took the other one, too. It looked like a jumping-jack and was about a foot tall.

McDowell followed the ghost out to the shadder of the barn. It would go ahead of McDowell and come back. McDowell said, "Tell me."

It said, "My wife and my farm."

Mrs. Ernshaw had followed McDowell and heard the ghost say, "My wife and my farm." She halloed, and it disappeared.

McDowell had come to find out what the ghost was. It had been bothering for some time.

*　　*　　*

Ghosts in this last group of tales appear to warn of a threatening danger or of impending death, or they appear to give notice that death has already occurred. In these tales the important thing is not the apparition, but the warning or "token" that it gives. This warning need not even by given by a ghost. In one brief story a sick man found his doom presaged in the hooting of an owl; in another a mother is warned of the death of her sons by the screaming of a cat and the clanking of chains.

*　　*　　*

54

THE FRALEY GHOST[22]

My father used to live in a double log house that was called the Fraley Place. People who lived there said that at night one would hear a voice saying, "Hello!" and footsteps coming up to the door, but when they went to the door no one would be there.

One night Father heard the voice and footsteps twice. The first time he got up and went to the door, but he couldn't see anything. He went back to bed and went to sleep. The voice yelled again. Father went back again and found that an old-fashion rail fence was on fire.

55
THE VINGARD WARNING[23]

Ernest Vingard was coming home one night and saw a casket come in front of him. It followed him and kept right on following him. He told a couple of his friends. They told him to ask it what it wanted. But the casket wouldn't tell him as long as anybody was with him. He went off a little way from his friends, and the casket changed into a little man. It told him that two fellows would come to his house to get him to go to a dance but he mustn't go, for they would kill him. Sure enough two fellows did come by one night and begged him to go to a dance, but he wouldn't go. At the dance there was a drunken fight, and some men were hurt.

56
THE IRVING GRAVEYARD GHOST[24]

Clem Mosley saw a ghost one night when he had been to see Sophia Sharpe, who became his third wife. Clem left Old Man Sharpe's place, riding a mule. He rode down a lane to the main road and got down to open the gate. He looked up above the trees and saw a white object, about the size of a bolster, floating. He got on his mule and the white object floated along before him. Once it disappeared, but soon he saw it again.

When Clem came to Scott Harmon's place, he was so scared that he would have stayed all night, but he couldn't think of a good excuse. He rode on with the object floating on ahead. He came to Mrs. Mosley's barn. He jerked the saddle off. The figure was still there. He grabbed the bridle and the figure floated off to Irving Graveyard not far away and sank down and disappeared.

Years later when Sophia Mosley died, she was buried at the exact spot that Clem saw the figure disappear.

57

THE HOOT-OWL[25]

When my first husband died, we lived in the country north of Carterville. While he was sick, a hoot-owl came and lit on the steps of the porch outside and hollered three times. It stood with its head toward the porch. The hooting aroused my husband, and he said to me, "That's my call." I didn't ask any questions. He died. His name was Tom Spiller.

58

CHAT GARLA[26]

There's a story about the old Governor Bond property. When the river washed Kaskaskia away, they tore the old Bond House down and moved it to the island. Folks claimed that it was a hainted house. It was a big house with lots of rooms, and it would hold a lot of people. A woman and her two sons once lived there. She was a widow.

The oldest boy wanted to go hunting one day, but she wouldn't let him go because it was All Souls' Day. People believed that it was wrong to hunt on that day because they thought that the birds and animals might be the souls of dead people who had returned to earth. But the boy stole the gun and slipped out of the house with it. He had hitched the team to the wagon to get some wood. When he was climbing over the fence with the gun, it went off and killed him. The gun scared the team and it started to running away. The younger boy fell out and was drug to death.

The chain traces made a rattling noise, and a black cat at the house ran upstairs screaming. The woman said that she knew that something had happened, for

she heard the cat and the chains. She always said that
the cat had warned her.

After that, people on the island wouldn't go hunting
or fishing on All Souls' Day because they said that
they were afraid of the *Chat garla*. People who lived at
the Bond House after that said that they heard noises
of a cat screaming and of chains rattling.

59

JOHN HENSON'S SPIRIT

A²⁷

The minister over at Saline River saw something one
time that is hard to explain. Dutton was his name.
I've known him ever since he was a boy. He is a con-
scientious, truthful and upright man. John Henson was
a young fellow who lived in the same community that
Dutton lived in. They were companions. I knew John,
too, when he was about seventeen or eighteen.

One night Dutton was walking home. He saw John
on a hill three-quarters of a mile from home. John was
coming down the hill toward Dutton. Dutton walked
up to John and said, "Hello! Where are you going?"
When he had done that the apparition went straight
up and disappeared.

Dutton started down the road home, and he ran all
the way. He ran through the gate at home and onto
the porch, waking the folks up. When he got in the
house he lit a lamp and let it burn all night.

He had awakened his folks when he came in, and
the next morning his father asked him about it. He
told him what he'd seen. His father tried to make him
think that he'd had a hallucination, but he couldn't
convince Dutton.

About a month later John Henson suddenly took

sick and died. Dutton always said that it was John's spirit he had met that night. You couldn't convince him of anything else.

I heard a fellow tell this one time. He's younger than I am, but reliable. He said that Will Dutton was riding home one night past the Potts Place. He looked up the road and seen one of his boy friends come walking down the road. Dutton said, "Hi." His friend began to go around in circles, each time getting higher and higher up in the air, and finally disappeared. It scared Dutton, and he run his horse home. About three weeks later his friend, a man named Henson, died.

60

THE SICK MAN'S GHOST²⁹

Father told me this story. This experience, and another one he had, had a great influence on his life.

Father was in the Civil War. He was pretty young when he joined the army. He fell in with tough companions, and soon he became pretty rough. The men were infidels, and they made a convert of Father.

After the war Father worked for an old gentleman named Jonathan Froman. Everybody called him Uncle Jonathan. Uncle Jonathan was a fairly wealthy man and pretty widely read.

One time church was going on in the settlement a little way from Uncle Jonathan's. One night during the meeting a frolic was held in the same settlement. Father decided to go to the dance instead of going to church. On his way to the dance he had to pass a farm where an old gentleman was bad sick. This old man had a son about Father's age.

On passing the farm of the sick man, coming from the dance, Father saw a fellow walking down through the field. Father thought it was the old man's son, and he slowed down. He thought the son had been to church, and Father thought he would ask what had happened at church and who was there, like a young fellow will. But just before the son got in speaking distance to him, that fellow turned a little to one side and went over a fence, and he didn't climb or jump the fence. It just seemed that he walked down, raised up in air as he was walking, crossed over the fence, and sank down to the ground on the other side.

Some cattle were grazing along there. They became very much excited and came running down to where Father was. Father turned his eyes to the cattle for a moment, and when he looked back, he couldn't see the man any more. The cattle ran on down on the inside of the fence near Father. It seemed that they wanted companionship. They weren't afraid of Father, but they were afriad of the apparition.

Father said that he talked to old Uncle Jonathan Froman about what he'd seen. Uncle Jonathan said that he had seen the sick man's spirit. "He'll die," said Uncle Jonathan, "and you'll see it." Uncle Jonathan's belief in ghosts was that you can see a man's spirit before he dies but never after. On death the spirit leaves this world never to return.

Sure enough, Father said, the fellow died in the course of about a week.

Father talked about it as long as he lived. It kind of had a bearing on his infidelity. It proved to him that man had a spirit apart from the body. It was no hallucination of Father's. Father wasn't even frightened. He just thought that the man's son was walking down to meet him to tell him something. If Father had seen it alone, he might have thought it was a hallucination, but the cattle saw it, too.

He didn't see it again, and the cattle didn't either, for they turned their heads and looked.

61

THE McCONNALL BANSHEE[30]

Before any one of the McConnell family died, a benshee (*sic*) would scream, and it would take the route that the family would go to the cemetery. The neighbors along the route would hear it.

When old lady Brown died—she was a McConnall—the banshee came into the house and got in bed. It looked like a little old woman about a foot high, with a rag tied around its head. John Gentry[31] was going to kill it, but Mrs. Brown said, "Don't bother that. That's my baby."

Some folks said that the benshee was a curse sent by the church, for the McConnalls had once burned a church.

When Walter Fraley's baby died, the benshee cried all over the place, but no one could see it.

62

THE GHOST AT THE FIREPLACE[32]

Father had another experience that greatly affected his life. He had a sister-in-law, named Mary, who had a spell of fever. I guess it was typhoid. She got to be pretty bad, and father and mother had been over there about two days and two nights.

Father's younger brother was at our home, taking care of things while they were gone.

After Father and Mother had sat up there about two nights, they came home. They thought that my aunt was better; she seemed to be resting well. They came home to get some sleep. When they got there, .they found that Father's brother had finished feeding and had gone off somewhere. Father built up the fire in the fireplace, and Mother got supper. They were both sleepy, and they got ready to go to bed early, but before going to bed Father covered up the fire.

Away late in the night Father heard some one poking the fire. He thought it was his brother. It woke him up slightly. The fire blazed up brightly. He could see it like a man can see the fire through the lids of his eyes. And he turned over and opened his eyes, intending to ask his brother where he'd been. When he looked in the room, he could see only the still glow of the fire, and no one was there. He hadn't heard a move other than the punching of the fire. No one had gone out of the room, and the doors of the house were shut. Father got up and looked at the fire. It was almost as he had left it. There was a little glow. The iron poker was just as he had left it, and he had heard some one pick up an iron poker and lay it down. He had heard distinctly the ring on the rocks. Father looked at the clock. It was three.

It worried him a little. He didn't know what to think, but he didn't wake Mother. She'd lost a lot of sleep and was tired. When he went back to bed he was soon asleep, for he had lost a great deal of sleep.

About daybreak some one rode up to the house and holloed, "Hello!" Father got up and went to the door. A man was there on horseback. He told Father that Mary had died that morning at three o'clock.

NOTES ON CHAPTER V

1. Related by Mrs. Ollie Barnard, Shawneetown. The Barnard and Lowry families—Mrs. Barnard was a Lowry before her marriage—tell a number of ghost-stories, some of which concern their own relatives and ancestors. Certain members of the family believe in ghosts, and all of them like tales of a ghostly character.

2. Told by Miss Thelma Barnard, Shawneetown, a daughter of Mrs. Ollie Barnard.

3. Mr. Gordon Lowry, Shawneetown, brother of Mrs. Barnard, related this incident, which he had learned from a certain Edward Penell.

4. Miss Esther Knefelkamp, Belleville, gave me this story, which she had learned from Mrs. Grace Robbs, also of Belleville, who had heard it at neighborhood gatherings when she was a child. As a result of hearing such stories in her child-

hood, Mrs. Robbs said that she was years overcoming her fear of the dark, ghosts, and haunted houses. This tale is an example of a ghost-story which has been preserved in an industrial city.

Stith Thompson mentions examples of magic wallets or sacks from which one cannot escape in his *Motif-Index of Folk Literature*, (Helsinki, 1932–1936; F. F. Comm. 106–109, 116–117) vol. II, p. 200, D1413.12. He also cites a number of examples of ghosts haunting houses, *ibid.*, p. 361, E281.

5. See Story No. 43, p. 74.

6. Related by Mr. Gordon Lowry, Shawneetown. This is a family story, in which certain members of the family seem to place credence.

Thompson records the fact that a number of stories have been built around mysterious ghostlike noises, *Motif-Index*, vol. II, p. 369, E402. See likewise Kittridge's *Witchcraft in Old and New England*, (Cambridge [Mass.], 1929) p. 214. Thompson also finds stories in which the ghost is laid by prayer, *ibid.*, p. 380, E443.

7. Told by Mr. Gordon Lowry, Shawneetown. See Note 6 above.

Tales of ghosts haunting houses are numerous; Thompson lists a number of such stories, *ibid.*, vol. II, pp. 361–362, E281. Thompson also lists stories in which ghostly noises are heard, such as footsteps, *ibid.*, vol. II, p. 369, E402.

8. Mr. Gordon Lowry, Shawneetown, likewise related this tale.

9. Related by Miss Esther Knefelkamp, Belleville, who obtained the story from Mrs. Grace Robbs, also of Belleville. See Note 4 above. A ghostly wagon appears in another tale of this collection: Story No. 48, pp. 80–81. Thompson, *ibid.*, gives an instance of a ghost appearing as a glowing wagon, vol. II, E421.3.5.

10. Mr. E. N. Hall, Elizabethtown, told this story. At the time I met him, in the summer of 1928, he was serving as county superintendent of schools in Hardin County. He had been a minister, an editor of the local paper, a teacher, and a farmer.

The incident in this story, of the ghost easily keeping pace with a running team, suggests the similar feat of "the Dug Hill Boger" in Story No. 45, pp. 75–77.

11. Told by Mr. John H. Treece, Jonesboro. The scene of this story is the Dug Hill Neighborhood west of Jonesboro. Among the inhabitants of that neighborhood, there is a fairly wide-spread belief that Dug Hill is haunted. A number of them believe that they have seen apparitions of some kind. One woman is supposed to have seen a lighted taper floating before her as she was going through the pass after sunset. Story No. 14, pp. 31–33 suggests the possible origin of the Dug Hill apparition.

12. Related by Mr. E. N. Hall, Elizabethtown. See Note 10 above. In a number of European ghost stories the apparition appears as a dog, Thompson, *ibid.*, vol. II, p. 373, E421 and p. 375, E423.1.1.

13. Mr. E. N. Hall, Elizabethtown, is also the narrator of this tale. See Note 10 above. This story appears to have a fairly wide circulation in Hardin County, perhaps because so many people have seen or heard this apparition. The fact that the ghost appears in three different guises would, no doubt, partly explain its being so well known.

Ghosts frequently appear in these three guises. See Notes 4, 6, and 12 above.

14. Mr. John H. Treece, Jonesboro, gave me the story of the flying wagon. See Note 11 above. The scene of this story is the same as that of *The Dug Hill Boger*, pp. 74–76. *The Flying Wagon*, too, is pretty generally known in the Dug Hill Neighborhood.

Magic air journeys are used frequently in folk-tales. Thompson lists a good many, *ibid.*, vol. II, p. 320, D2135. He lists an example of ghosts in a glowing wagon, E421.3.5. A number of the wild hunt stories contain horses: p. 392, E501.4.2, ff. In some of these stories the wild hunt is heralded by the noise of chains, p. 396, E501.13.1.2, and by the noise of horses, p. 396, E501.13.3, f. And still another wild hunt story tells how the hunt disappeared with the movement of the tree-tops, p. 398, E501.16.2.

15. Told by Mr. E. N. Hall, Elizabethtown. See Note 10 above. Story No. 33, p. 58 also deals with a mineral light, but in the case of this story the narrator assumes that the light is a mineral light rather than an apparition.

Luminous ghosts are relatively numerous in folk tales. Thompson lists twelve or more examples, *ibid.*, vol. II, p. 373, E421.3 and f. and E7402.2, p. 423.

16. Related by Mr. Charles Neely, Sr., Carbondale. This story Mr. Neely heard in his childhood, and it seems to have been widely known in the southern part of Pope County.

The fear test is popular in folk-tales. Thompson lists a number of tests: a man stays in a haunted house, *ibid.*, vol. III, p. 398, H1411; staying in haunted house where corpse drops piecemeal down chimney, p. 398, H1411.1. As a result of his bravery the man is rewarded with money, *ibid.*, vol. II, p. 367, E373.1.

17. Told by Mr. Carl Wynn, Carterville. The story was brought from Tennessee and handed down in the Wynn family.

18. This variant was related by Mrs. Mary U. Stallion, Elizabethtown. Mrs. Stallion's family also came from Tennessee, but this story is told as if the incident had happened in Hardin County, Illinois.

19. Obtained from the late Isaac J. Hartline, Carbondale. See Note 5, p. 39. This is a family story.

Thompson lists an example of the dead returning to demand stolen property, *ibid.*, vol. II, p. 357, E236.

20. Secured from Miss Millie Barnard, Shawneetown, daughter of Mrs. Ollie Barnard. See Note 1 above.

The return of a dead spouse to remonstrate with an erring partner is a well-known folk-lore motif. Thompson mentions a number of stories with such a motif: *ibid.*, vol. II, pp. 354–355, E221 and E221.1. Child II, 281, No. 86.

21. Related by Mr. Gordon Lowry, Shawneetown. See Notes 3 and 20 above. Kittredge, op. cit., p. 217 gives examples of the pulling off of bed-clothing.

22. Told by Mr. Gordon Lowry, Shawneetown.

23. Told by Mr. Gordon Lowry, Shawneetown. Thompson lists a number of stories in which the dead return from the grave to give counsel: *ibid.*, vol. II, p. 366. E366.

24. Secured from the late Mrs. Julia M. Bell, Carbondale. See Note 19, p. 41, and Note 4 above.

25. Obtained from Mrs. Lizzie Toler, Carbondale.

26. Related by Mrs. Mary Louise Garner, Kaskaskia. See Note 11, p. 40.

27. Mr. E. N. Hall, Elizabethtown, told this story. See Note 10 above. The tale seems to be fairly well known in Hardin County.

Thompson does not mention an example of the soul's leaving the body shortly before death, though he does mention a number of stories in which the soul leaves the body; *ibid.*, vol. II, pp. 418–420.

28. Mr. Gordon Lowry, Shawneetown, related this variant of Story 59. It seems fair to assume that the tale is pretty well known in Hardin County and southern Gallatan.

29. Secured from Mr. E. N. Hall, Elizabethtown. See Note 10 above. The theme of this story is practically the same as that in Story 59.

30. Obtained from Mr. Gordon Lowry, Shawneetown. The banshee is a household spirit belonging to certain families. This superstition is frequently found in Ireland.

31. See Note 13, p. 60.

32. Related by Mr. E. N. Hall, Elizabethtown. Thompson, *ibid.*, vol. II, p. 419, E722. Lowry C. Wimberly, *Folklore in the English and Scottish Ballads*, (Chicago, 1928), p. 268.

CHAPTER VI

WITCHCRAFT

WITCHES are less common than ghosts in the folk-tales of Egypt, but witchcraft is firmly woven into the folk heritage. Sometimes it appears in stories with well-defined witchcraft motifs such as sympathetic magic and transformation. Often it appears as superstitions, usually involving magic. Belief in magic explains the superstition that a snake cannot die until sunset, no matter how horribly beaten and mangled it may be. The most common superstitions of this kind concern the dairy. Farm-boys in some sections of Egypt are taught never to kill toads lest the cows give bloody milk. But when cows do give bloody milk, the remedy is very simple: one has only to hold a bucket of the milk over the flames of a fireplace and whip it into the fire with thorn switches. When butter fails to come after persistent churning, the housewife knows that the cream is bewitched. To break the spell, she must put a gold coin in the bottom of the churn, an American adaptation of the old English counter-charm of placing a shilling or a crooked sixpence in the churn.[1]

Most story-tellers are not concerned with the problem of how one may become a witch. One story, however, answers the question. "My great-grandmother," a woman told me once, "Wanted to be a witch when she was young. A woman told her that she must sell her soul to the devil to become a witch. This woman had her say, 'I belong to the devil and no one else.' She began saying it, and it began to grow dark. My great-grandmother got scared and said, 'O, my God!' It got light then, and the witch said, 'You've played it now'!"[2]

Tales of witchcraft are not peculiar to any one section

of Egypt but are pretty generally dispersed throughout the region. The stories in this chapter come from Gallatin and Pope counties along the Ohio River, from Jackson County in the western central part of the section, and from St. Clair in the northwest. These tales were all told by white people who are descendants of settlers from the older states and from Germany.

*   *   *

Transformation alone is a rather uncommon motif; generally it is associated with magic. In two of the stories which follow, transformation is the sole motif; in the other it is coupled with disenchantment by shooting. One of them comes from Pope County on the Ohio River and the other two from Jackson. All tales can be traced to a fairly early date. The two Jackson County stories go back to the grandmother of a man now in his eighties, the one from Pope to an early settler who was part Indian.

63

THE WOMAN WHO WAS A DEER[3]

In the Alcorn Creek neighborhood in Pope County, people believed in witches. Uncle Wesley Holt, who was an old settler and part Indian, saw a deer galloping around the field. Being an expert marksman with the old cap and ball rifle, Uncle Wesley decided to have some venison. He shot at the deer and it galloped away. For several days it galloped around the field. Uncle Wesley shot at it several times but failed to kill it.

He knew that his marksmanship was good, so he decided that there was something uncanny about the deer. Understanding witchcraft, he decided to try another method. This method was to drill a hole through the lead ball, cut a piece of silver from a dime, and insert it in the hole. He loaded his gun and killed the deer at the first shot. When he came to the deer, it turned out to be old Mary Toombs, who was a witch in the neighborhood.

64

THE MAN WHO WAS A HORSE[4]

There was a man named Jacobs who lived neighbor to my grandmother. He weighed about one hundred and eighty pounds. One summer he commenced to fall off, and he wasn't sick. There had to be some cause. Folks asked him finally what was the matter. He said that some one in the neighborhood turned him into a big bay horse every night and rode him hard but wouldn't give him any hay or corn. The man said that he was a pretty horse.

My grandmother told me this story.

"Grandma, that couldn't be," I said.

"That's what he said about it," Grandma said.

65

THE CAT IN THE FIREPLACE[5]

My grandmother stayed with us while my father was in the army. One evening she went over to a neighbor's house, and they all sat by the fireplace. The children were all in bed. While they set there talking, they heard a noise in the chimney that sounded like a cat, and pretty soon a cat fell into the fire. The next day one of the neighbor women showed burns. She was a witch and had turned herself into a cat.

I says, "Grandma, you don't believe that. Can't no women turn herself into a cat."

And she says to me, "Johnny, you don't know what to believe."

* * *

In the next story two motifs explicitly appear—transformation and sympathetic magic, and a third one is implied—magic transportation.

* * *

66

THE WITCH WHO STOLE MILK[6]

Once upon a time there was an old woman living on a farm. The neighbors said that she was a witch. This old woman moved from her place to her son's some distance away. In those days the neighbors helped do the moving. The old woman had a high-backed rocker on her front porch, and she was seen sitting there very often. When one of the last movers saw her sitting on her front porch, rocking to and fro, he asked her if he could not take her and her rocker along as it was some distance to her new home. Then the old lady said, "Oh, no, my boy. I and my rocker will be there ahead of you-all." And lo and behold, when the wagon arrived at the new home, the old lady was calmly rocking on the front porch of her new home.

After a time everybody's cows in that neighborhood gave no milk. This old lady had several towels hanging on her back porch. With a towel hanging before her, she would milk the neighbors' cows from the lower two corners; when she was finished she would have several large foaming buckets of wholesome milk. This same lady used to bewitch the neighbors' horses and make them sick. They would see a black shadow, and when they go to the barn they would see a cat. The son took a shot at her. The next morning the old lady's hands were all crippled up. At another time this old lady went into another's corn crib to steal corn. Some one of the boys decided to take a shot at her. He didn't kill her, just crippled her. So he took a dime and broke it into pieces and used that for a shot. A black cat ran away meowing like the devil. The next day some one called on her. The old woman had to stay in bed, for she was all shot up, and blood was trickling in streams down her face.   *   *   *

Magic pure and simple is the motif of the next five stories; in some of them it is black magic, in others white. Magical power is at the command of a farmer in one of the stories because he owns the Sixth and Seventh Books of Genesis—a circumstance which suggests certain European folk-tales, though in them it is usually the gospel of a saint or a prayer-book that gives the supernatural power.

                    *   *   *

67

THE WREATH IN THE PILLOW[7]

Doctors seemed to be at loss as to just what was troubling Clarence Manners. The child had been ill for a period of five weeks, getting weaker day by day.

One day a neighbor came in to see Clarence and told his mother doctors could do the child little good, for he was bewitched. She suggested they look into the pillow upon which Clarence rested his head. Upon opening the pillow a wreath formed by the feathers was found. The wreath was not entirely finished, the neighbor explained, and for that reason Clarence was still alive. At the suggestion of the neighbor the wreath was placed on a chair and a rope was used to beat it until it was demolished.

The next day an old lady living in the neighborhood was confined to her bed with a bruised body. Mrs. Manners realized then that it was she who had bewitched her son. Clarence recovered soon after the wreath was destroyed.

68

THE DRIED FOOT-PRINT[8]

Once upon a time there was a farmer who planted seventy-five acres of young fruit trees. The next morning all of the trees were pulled up. He asked his hired man to replant the trees. Again the trees were pulled up. Then the third time the farmer told his hired man to plow and harrow the ground well so that not a foot-print could be seen. The hired man did this, and the third time the trees were pulled up.

This time the farmer found a foot-print near one of the trees. As carefully as he could he carried the ground with the foot-print to the house and very slowly began to dry the ground. He had his suspicions, and since he owned the Sixth and Seventh Books of Genesis and therefore had magical powers, he felt that he could find the culprit. He said, "The fellow who did this will get sick." He let the ground with the foot-print dry for several days, and then he went to the house of the man he suspected. The man was very sick in bed. The farmer left and returned the next day. The fellow was worse the next day, and his family thought he was dying. The farmer said that when the foot-print was thoroughly dry, the fellow would die. The fellow promised never to do it again, and the farmer let him go.

69

KILLING A WITCH[9]

Uncle Charles Lowry was accused of killing a witch one time. A witch in the neighborhood bewitched him. Some one told him to put a needle under the hearth and burn it. He got a needle and put it under the hearth. The witch sent over to his house to borrow a needle. He wouldn't let her have it. She sent for him and wanted to borrow a needle to pick her teeth. He refused and she died.

70

BREAKING A WITCH'S CHARM[10]

Uncle Wesley Holt was sick with chills and fever.[11] Medicine would do him no good. He decided at last that Old Man Toombs, the husband of Mary Toombs, had bewitched him. To break the charm he drew a picture of Toombs and shot at it with a lead ball and missed the picture. Then he bored a hole through a ball and inserted a piece of silver. Then he shot again and hit the picture between the knee and the ankle. A few minutes later one of the Toombs children came over to borrow some coffee. He refused because to borrow something would break the charm. After that Old Man Toombs was afflicted with a sore on his shin as long as he lived.

71

THE BEWITCHED COLT[12]

She told me another story—a story about a man that had a filly colt.[13] They was a man named James Smith. He went out to the barn one morning and found the colt down. She kicked when he tried to help her up. There was a man in the neighborhood who could cure the colt, and Smith had him come over.

This man had them all go in the kitchen. He told the women to take the dishes and the cloth off. He turned the table around and cut notches in it. He said for no one to say anything because the witch was coming, man or woman he didn't know which. Soon a woman came and wanted to borrow something. This man said everything to her. Finally, one of the men in the room said, "Haven't you said enough to her?"

The man said, "Why didn't you keep quiet? I almost had the spell broken. Now the horse will never be right. It will get well, but there will always be something wrong with it."

Neighbors kept watch on the colt. When it got up it was four inches lower in front than behind.

*   *   *

In this last story the same farmer who owned the Sixth and Seventh Books of Genesis exercised his magical powers, in some occult fashion, to trap a thief. His method, however, is not revealed.

*   *   *

72

THE THIEF WITH THE SACK OF WHEAT[14]

This same farmer (the one with the Sixth and Seventh Books of Genesis) who used magic was the envy of all his neighbors because he had plentiful wheat crops. One morning when his son went to feed the horses, he found a man standing stock still, holding a wheat-sack. He could not move. The boy said, "Good morning." The man wouldn't speak. The boy rushed to tell the family, who were ready to eat breakfast. The father said, "I know—he's been standing there since two o'clock this morning. Go and see if his wagon and team are behind the barn." The son obeyed and found five sacks of wheat on the man's wagon.

The farmer went to the barn. He told the man that he should go to his wagon and return the sacks of wheat he had taken. The man did this. Then the farmer invited him in to eat breakfast. The man promised the farmer that he would never come back, and he never did.

NOTES TO CHAPTER VI

1. George Lyman Kittredge, *Witchcraft in Old and New England* (Cambridge [Mass.], 1929) p. 167.

2. Related by Mrs. Ollie Barnard, Shawneetown. See Note 1, p. 97.

Thompson in *Motif-Index of Folk-Literature* lists several stories in which magic power is obtained from the devil, vol. II, p. 72, D812.3 Kittredge also discusses compact with Satan, *op. cit.*, pp. 239 ff. L. C. Wimberly likewise mentions the traditional compact between the devil and witches in *Folklore in the English and Scottish Ballads*, p. 357.

3. Secured from Mr. Charles Neely, Sr., Carbondale, who heard it when he was a boy living in the southern part of Pope County. The story was an old wives' tale that was pretty generally known in that section.

For examples of disenchantment by shooting, see Thompson *op. cit.*, p. 62, D712.7. Kittredge, *op. cit.*, p. 92, mentions an example of the use of a silver bullet to break a spell.

Several stories of transformttion of a man to a deer are listed in Thompson, *op. cit.*, p. 14, D114.1.

4. Told by Mr. John Crashaw, Carbondale, who learned this story from his grandmother. It is not generally known in the community in which Mr. Crashaw lives.

Thompson, *ibid.*, p. 15, D131 and vol. III, G241.2.1. has recorded many examples of the transformation of man to a horse. The motif appears not only in Germanic folk-tales, but also in Slavic and Hindu stories as well. Kittredge mentions the motif briefly in *op. cit.*, p. 219. In fact, the motif is almost a commonplace of witchcraft.

5. This tale likewise was obtained from Mr. John Crashaw, who heard his grandmother tell it when he was a boy.

See Thompson, *op. cit.*, p. 17, D142. He lists French and German, as well as American Indian stories with this motif. Kittredge, *op. cit.*, p. 177 ff., says that there are countless examples in modern stories in which a cat-witch, injured in that shape, suffers the same wound in her proper person.

6. Miss Esther Knefelkamp, Belleville, related this story which she had obtained from Mr. Henry Juenger, Sr., also of Belleville. Mr. Juenger believed his story, observing, "Years ago some women were witches and could take any form they pleased. This lady (the witch of the story) was my neighbor—I know. I was

the son who took a shot at her. This is not just a yarn; it really happened. It's so."

For references concerning the transformation motif in this story, see Note 5 above. Thompson, *op. cit.*, p. 225 and vol. III, G211.2 and D1520.16, lists an example of magic transformation by means of a chair; see also p. 123, D1151.2. and D142 of vol. II. Kittredge, *op. cit.*, pp. 163–166, gives instances of witches stealing milk, usually by means of a bag or sack.

7. Miss Irene Mache, Belleville, gave me this story, which she had obtained from Mrs. John Becker of Belleville.

Thompson, *op. cit.*, pp. 310–311, D2064, D2064.2, gives stories in which sickness is caused by magic; in one tale the presence of a toad under a bed causes sickness, and in still another tale sickness is dependent upon a witch's fire.

8. Obtained by Miss Esther Knefelkamp, Belleville, from Mrs. Louis Stein, who lives near Belleville.

In many folk-tales magic power rests in a person by virtue of his possessing sacred books; see Thompson, *ibid.*, p. 142, D1266 and D1266.1 and Vol. VI, V151, and Kittredge, *op. cit.*, p. 146, 465 nn. 66, 67, 70.

In European tales witchcraft is often wrought by drying sod bearing the footprint of an individual over a fire. As the sod dries, the individual suffers from a withered foot: Kittredge, *ibid.*, p. 102. Sir James G. Frazer mentions numerous examples of the same sort of magic among more primitive peoples, as well as among Europeans: see *The Golden Bough*[3], (London, 1911) vol. I, pp. 207–211. I have met the same superstition in Southern Illinois; there is a belief current in certain sections that one may cause a person to have a headache by stepping in his footprint.

9. Secured from Mrs. Ollie Barnard, Shawneetown; this is a family story.

Many folk-tales contain examples of murder by magic; an object or an animal is abused or destroyed to bring about the death of a person: Thompson, *op. cit.*, p. 309, D2061.2.2. As a counter-charm to witchcraft, pins are heated in a bottle on the theory that the pins will prick the heart of the witch; see Kittredge, *op. cit.*, p. 102, 411 ff. nn. 1–171.

10. Told by Mr. Charles Neely, Sr., Carbondale. This tale was current in the southern part of Pope County a number of years ago.

Kittredge devotes a chapter to the discussion of image magic (*Ibid.*, Chapter III, pp. 73–103), and he mentions examples of this type of magic in North Carolina, Nova Scotia, Elizabethan England, p. 92. Frazer, *op. cit.*, pp. 55 ff. has collected numerous examples of image magic among the American Indians and other savage people of the world, among the Chinese, Japanese, and Hindus, among ancient people and among the Highlanders of Scotland.

11. See Story 63, pp. 102–103.

12. Related by Mr. John Crashaw, Carbondale. See Note 4, p. 109.

Kittredge tells of the use of white witchcraft to cure disease among human beings and animals, *op. cit.*, pp. 30–31, 96–97, but mentions no case exactly parallel to the one in this story.

13. Mr. John Crashaw's grandmother; see Note 4, p. 109.

14. Obtained by Miss Esther Knefelkamp, Belleville, from Mrs. Louis Stein, who lives near Belleville. See Note 8 above.

CHAPTER VII

TREASURE-TROVES

INTEREST in treasure-troves is fairly common in Egypt, particularly among people of broken fortunes or with no expectations. Negroes are often persistent diggers for treasure-troves and likewise countryfolk living in the isolated and poverty-stricken regions of the Ozark Hills. On rare occasions one may find a local antiquary who tells stories of lost or buried wealth because of the distinction that these tales bring to the neighborhood.

As a rule, the basis for belief in treasure-troves is astonishingly slim. There is no record that precious metals have ever been mined in Egypt or that great fortunes have ever been concealed. Yet the legends of lost wealth persist, and people continue to dig. In certain sections the search is for a lost gold or silver mine which was known to the Indians and perhaps to the Spanish expeditions, believed by some people to have visited a number of regions in Egypt. At the cave in Cave-in-Rock, numerous excavators have hoped to unearth a portion of the ill-gotten gold of the river pirates. In most cases, however, the searchers have sought the miser's pot of gold, or gold hidden away during the turbulent days of the Civil War.

Some searchers make use of mineral rods to locate the trove; in one instance a negro claimed to have been directed by the voice of a spirit. He also searched his Bible for clues of buried wealth. Most seekers had no other guide than old wives' tales.

Although in some stories one gathers that a trove has been unearthed, there is almost never an eye-witness. The treasure-seekers, strangers as a rule, disappear as mysteriously as they come without a word to anyone, leaving behind an excavated place in which one may see the imprint of a pot or kettle.

*   *   *

73

SNAKES IN THE HOLE[1]

Uncle Tom Kaylor was a wizard, people said. People in the neighborhood used to go to him when their milk wouldn't make butter. Uncle Tom would tell them to melt a piece of silver. Uncle Tom also had a mineral rod with which he located buried treasure.

It was believed among the people of that community that money was buried on Aunt 'Liza McGhee's place. Uncle Tom took his mineral rod one moonlight night and located the buried treasure. He marked the spot. The next night he hired a negro well-digger, old Bill Dotson, to dig down to the money.

They went to the place and Bill began to dig. It was fall and pretty cold. Bill got down a few feet and the snakes began to crawl out the sides of the hole and coil about Dotson's feet. The deeper Dotson dug, the more numerous the snakes were. Finally, Dotson couldn't stand it any longer. He pitched his spade out of the hole and climbed out.

If Kaylor ever went back to hunt the money, no one ever knew, but Dotson never went back.

74

THE SPILLER TREASURE-TROVE[2]

It seems to me it was Trab Gagus that first found out about the Spiller Treasure-trove. He was one of the diggers anyhow. And the others I don't know. He told me about it. He was one of the diggers and the boys he had was young. He explained to the boys about the wind. It must have been years back when he was young, for I have been here thirty-six years. I don't know how far back it was.

I don't know how they got wind of gold on the Spiller place, but one man, Jack Diamond, said a spirit told him. He said he was walking along, and he heard some one say, "There's gold buried here." He took his rod (mineral rod, I suppose), and went to hunt. Anyway he said it was just at the place. He hunted from the sound of the spirit. But he never found nothing.

I don't know how the other bunch heard about it. But anyway, Mr. Spiller said somebody was digging all over the place. He didn't bother them, but he said that some one was digging some terribly big holes.

The bunch that really dug for the treasure got so deep that they really located it. They had to dig at night. They got down to the pot and decided to rest till the next night. Mr. Spiller asked them, "Boys, what are you digging—hunting for gold?"

"Yes," they said.

"That's all right—if you can find anything."

Next night they started. It seems that Mr. Spiller had some bad dogs. The diggers must have been close to the house. They got the pot just ready to lift out. What they were looking for was a whirlwind.[3] That came at night. They had to hold their breath while they took the pot out. Right after the wind the dogs came tearing down. I reckon Mr. Spiller was watching, too. Here came three dogs, just a-tearing. Wasn't nothing to do but get out. The dogs chased them clear home.

The next day they went back to their diggings, and there was the place the pot was taken out.

They say that Mr. Spiller sent the gold to Washington. Anyway he got the pot, big or little.

The diggers left the pot until the next day. They said

there was only three shovels of dirt to be thrown out. All they got for their digging was the print of the pot.

75

THE LEGEND OF MILLER POND[4]

There is a legend about Miller Pond, which is over here about Wolf Lake. A good many years ago there was an old man who lived by the pond. In fact he gave his name to it. In the early days, much more than at the present time, the silver dollar was the medium of exchange in the whole country. And there was a lot of counterfeiting going on in this part of the state. This old man Miller lived in a remote section where few people lived. Once in a while he would come to town and buy the necessities of life, always paying for them with silver dollars. No one knew where he got his money.

At length it was discovered that he was counterfeiting silver dollars. He was arrested and brought to trial. At the trial one of the dollars was weighed, and they discovered that his dollars had more silver in them than the government-coined dollar. Consequently the Court had to turn the old man loose. While the Court was still assembled the old man pulled out a sack filled with dollars and paid his attorney.

The source of the old man's silver has remained a mystery to this very day. He told no one where he got it, and no one has ever been able to discover the place.

This country, of course, was filled with Indians before the coming of the white man. It is related that an old Indian chief once remarked that the white man had no judgment. If he had, he would be shoeing his horses with gold shoes. It has been said that a cave five miles west of Alto Pass is full of gold. The cave was sealed when the white man came to this country, and no one has been able to locate it, although many people have tried to.

A few years ago out in the neighborhood where this cave is thought to be located, a man was digging a well. When he got down into the ground some distance, he heard a peculiar moaning sound, which some people think the wind caused. The man, however, feared that he was near the lost cave, and that he was hearing the groans that came from dead Indians. He climbed out of the half-dug well and filled it up.

76

FIGURED ROCK TREASURE[5]

Well, long before the Civil War, Figured Rock was well known. People made regular trips to visit it. And a good many people came there hunting wealth, hoping to locate the treasure that was thought to be hid, but nobody ever found anything more than a few coins. On these figured hieroglyphics; there's a deer with a dog after it and an Indian with a bow and arrow after the dog. I guess that made sense to the Indian, and he knew how to read it, but nobody today can. One corner of the rock is covered with Spanish writing. Some people have claimed they can read it. You won't find much on the rock nowadays. People have marked on it and chipped and the weather has wore it away.

Old Mike Swarthscope, who used to be County Surveyor of this county, was among the men who said he could read it. He used to stay out at Denny Cornor's a great deal of the time; he had a room there, and he'd draw maps of this country. He used to go often to Figured Rock and try to decipher the hieroglyphics. He couldn't make much headway, so he sent to St. Louis for two men. They came down and stayed for about two weeks, working over at the Figured Rock and staying at Denny's. Finally they went away. What they made of it I don't know, but I do know that people have claimed to read the Spanish part.

In that time Figured Rock was a noted place. Lots of people have visited it.

Superstition has it that the Indians put the letters there giving a history of their treasure. No one has ever been able to find them. Personally I don't believe they are there. But not many years ago an Indian woman died in Anna. She was a Cherokee Indian. She'd come to this country hunting for hidden treasure. By the description she gave of the place, people thought she had Figured Rock in mind.

77

THE ARNOLD TROVE[6]

Several years ago while we was in business at Pomona, a couple of strangers came to this country. Nobody knew who they were or where they came from. They stayed at John Cornon's. The men came down to the store and bought a grubbing-hoe and a spade, but the didn't say what they wanted with them. They'd take the hoe and spade and be gone the whole day, coming in at night. They'd been there about two days, and one evening they didn't show up. John got alarmed and he and his boy went out hunting for them. They didn't find the men, but they found the grubbing-hoe and the spade under an old apple-tree that they'd dug up. The tree was in old Arnold's field. Old Arnold was a very wealthy man. They saw four jars, and they were empty, but you could see where the coins had been in them. The two men were never heard of again.

78

THE KETTLE OF GOLD[7]

I have a story in mind which is true, and I shall relate it as I remember it.

Before we came to this town, we lived on a farm west of Ozark. This section of the country happens to be very rocky and contains several large bluffs. One of these chains of bluffs was just below our house, and we often played on them and made playhouses. There was a smooth upright bluff about ten feet high and on it was carved the picture of as natural a looking snake as was ever drawn. It was a rattle-snake and could be seen there until yet. The head of the snake was pointing due west with some figures under it. Just a few feet west of this was a projection of rock about six or seven feet long and a few feet wide. The rock was only about two feet thick at the edge of it. There was a round boulder lying on this about three feet in diameter and dirt was packed all around with moss growing on it. This made the smooth round rock look beautiful and also afforded a very pleasant seat. I have sat on the rock many times when we were playing there.

In the spring before we came here (Carterville) three strangers came and asked leave of the owner to prospect a little. Just in a little while they came back and wanted to buy the place and offered the owner about five times the worth of it. This excited the owner, and he would not sell it. So the men leased it for a few dollars to search for oil, as they said. They put them up a tent and began to dig a hole in the ground that day just for deception.

That night they searched for the treasure and found it. The next day they burned their tent and left.

When we went down to the bluff to see how they were getting along, we found the round stone rolled away and a hole chiseled out in the lower rock a foot and a half in diameter. You could see the prints of a kettle that had been in the hollow. There was also a round hole an inch or more in diameter drilled on through the rock. This was a drainage for the water. This kettle was full of gold and other valuables that were buried during the Civil War.

This was one time I sat on a pot of gold and didn't know it.

79

THE MYSTERIOUS DR. LYLE[3]

Jonathan Belt and Ben Lavender were brothers-in-law. Jonathan was a brother of Logan Belt. One day a stranger came into this country. He said that his name was Dr. Lyle, but his coming was a mystery and his leaving was, too.

Dr. Lyle and Jonathan met at a dance. They had a difference that ended in a fight. Jonathan said to Dr. Lyle that he would kill him. Belts didn't allow anybody to cross them.

Dr. Lyle claimed that he was a physician. I don't know whether he was or not. My father-in-law was down with a cancer, and Ben Lavender's mother was seriously sick. Dr. Lyle used to go see both of them. When people get in a hopeless condition they grab at every straw. I guess the doctor didn't do them much good.

One night Ben Lavender went over to see his mother. It was a cold night, and the ground was covered with snow. Ben saw the shadow of two guns on the snow, but he didn't see anybody. It gave him a leery feeling. He walked on up to the house and saw Jonathan Belt and his father, Jim Belt. Jim asked if Dr. Lyle was in the house. Ben said he didn't know, but he asked them not to make any disturbance because his mother was so low. The Belts insisted that they search the house. They said that they aimed to kill Lyle. Of course, Ben couldn't do anything. The Belts went in and searched the house. They caused a lot of disturbance but they didn't find Dr. Lyle. And nobody ever heard of Lyle again. I don't think he was killed. I think he slipped away.

When Lyle first landed here he told four or five men that he had a mission. He invited them all to go out with him to a cave where, he said, men had been counterfeiting. They all went with him out to a place not so far from here. The doctor kicked the dirt off of a rock, lifted the rock up, and revealed a cave with a beech-pole cut with prongs. It was called an Indian ladder. Lyle climbed down in the cave, but he didn't stay long. He came out and said: "Back up, back up if you don't want to be killed." He covered the cave up and said that the men down there had threatened his life. The men all went back to town.

The men who went out with Lyle were not satisfied. They went back the next day and opened the cave. They found a bellows and the cave was smoked from the furnace that had been used when the counterfeiting had been going on. But the cave hadn't been opened in years. Dr. Lyle evidently found what he wanted and tried to scare the men away.

80

THE GOLD BRICK[9]

One day two strangers came to Du Quoin. They inquired of farming people who would be likely to buy a gold brick. A merchant said that he knew a man—a bachelor with no family. The strangers hired a rig and went out. The strangers said to the farmer, "You've got a lot of money." The farmer said that he had a little but it was in the bank. They said that they had a gold brick that was worth twenty-five hundred dollars but that they would take fifteen hundred for it. They needed the money bad and wanted to sell. They unwrapped the brick and showed it to the farmer. The bachelor took a notion to own the brick. And the strangers told him that he would make a thousand dollars. The farmer felt of the brick and said that it was heavy enough to be worth fifteen hundred dollars. He wrote out a check and gave it to the men. Nobody ever heard of them again.

A few days later the bachelor went down to the bank and asked if the strangers had cashed his check. The banker said that they had. "Good," said the bachelor, for he was afraid that the strangers might want to trade back. He showed the brick to the banker, and he was afraid that the farmer had been soaked. He weighed it and persuaded the farmer to let him send the brick to Washington.

When the banker got the brick back, he found that one-half of it was ground glass and sand. He wrote the farmer a notice. The farmer hooked up then and there, and he broke down and cried. He had the banker clean the gold out and send it down to Washington. He got eight hundred dollars for his gold.

NOTES ON CHAPTER VII

1. Related by Mr. Charles Neely, Sr., Carbondale. This tale was formerly generally known in the southern part of Pope County. Tom Kaylor and Bill Dotson were both local "characters."

2. Told by Mr. Will Price, a Negro of Carbondale.

3. According to the narrator, Negro treasure-trove seekers believe that a whirlwind arises when they are ready to remove the trove.

4. Mr. Roy Wilkins, Alto Pass, told this story. He has long been interested in antiquarian lore in his neighborhood. He has collected treasure-trove stories, legends of Indians, and legends of the Spanish expeditions. He also owns a fair collection of Indian relics.

5. Secured from Mr. F. M. Reeves, Pamona. There seems to be a good deal of interest in the neighborhood in which Mr. Reeves lives concerning this lost wealth.

6. Related by Mr. F. M. Reeves, Pamona.

7. Miss Ruth Choate, Carterville, gave me this story.

8. Mrs. Rose, Elizabethtown, related this story.

9. Secured from Mr. John Crashaw, Carbondale.

CHAPTER VIII

EUROPEAN FOLK-TALES

FOLK-TALES with European motifs are by no means uncommon in Egypt, but European folk-tales in which something more than the motif has been preserved are somewhat rare. Preserved by a folk not many generations from the pioneer settlers, these stories have lost their richness of detail. Perhaps the details seemed a little strange, even exotic, to the pioneers. For some reason, these tales have never become thoroughly acclimated; they are distinctly not Egyptian, not even American, but are immigrants in an alien land.

In the case of the first story. "Why the Irish Came to America," the close resemblance between the Egyptian tale and the European original, the Swan Maiden story, can be accounted for by the fact that it passed through but two or three hands. The Irishman who told the story to the narrator or a friend of the narrator merely took a tale that he had learned in childhood and dressed it up to explain, in a fanciful way, why he had come to America.

"The Lame Man Recovers the Use of his Legs," on the other hand, seems to have come down to us by innumerable retellings. Consequently, it is poorer in detail than the first story.

*   *   *

81

HOW DEATH CAME TO IRELAND[1]

An Irishman told this story about a king of France. He said the King of France he wanted to get married, but he couldn't find no one that suited him. So he went

travelin' through the country huntin' a wife. He come
to a wilderness where an old hermit monk lived. The
king he stayed there awhile with the old monk, and
they'd go huntin'. One day they was out a-huntin' and
they saw three white swans. The king he wanted to kill
them, but the old monk he said: "No, don't kill them."
The king asked him why, and the old monk he said:
"They ain't swans. They're the girls who come to the
lake every day to swim." The old monk had lived a
thousand years, and he knew all about them things.

The king he wanted to catch the three girls. But the
old man said that the only way they could catch them
was to git their clothes, and that would be hard to do,
for the three women swam so fast that he couldn't git
the clothes. But the king kept on insistin' about catchin'
the three girls; so the old monk give him a pair of ten-
mile boots to put on. The king he put on the ten-mile
boots and slipped up the bank of the lake and stole the
three girl's clothes before they knowed it.

Then the girls swam to the shore where they saw
what the king had done, and they begged fer their
clothes. But the king wouldn't give them back without
they'd take him along with them. The three women
they agreed to. The oldest girl took the king first, and
she flew away with him, and her sisters followed. She
carried the king a long way till she came to a mountain,
and then she dropped him. The second sister she caught
him and carried him across the mountain and on a long
way till she got tired; then she dropped him. The youngest sister she caught the king and carried him the rest
of the way. She was the one the king was goin' to marry.

When they got to the home of the three sisters
though, the king he couldn't tell them apart, but the
youngest she give him a sign. She held her knees close
together, and the other two they held their knees
apart. And they were married and lived very happy.
But the king wanted to go back to France. His wife

told him that he couldn't, for he'd die if he did. He kept on insistin' on goin' back. His wife she fixed up a flying-ship to take him back, but she told him that he'd die if he got out. The king promised not to git out of the ship, but come right straight back.

When the king got to France, he forgot all about what he'd promised his wife. He stepped out on the ground and Death was right there, and he nabbed him.

"Don't take me, Death," the king said. "Take those old men around here, I'm young."

"I want you," said Death holdin' on tight to the king.

The king saw that Death was goin' to take him anyhow; so he said all right he'd go if Death would get in that box he had along also. Death got into the box, and the king slammed the lid shut and fastened it tight, so he couldn't git out. Then the king got in his machine and flew back to his wife.

When the king got back to his wife, he told her what had happened, and he started to open the box Death was in. His wife stopped him and said: "Don't open the box here. If you do, we'll all die."

They didn't know what to do with Death, but a big storm come up over the ocean, and they took the box with Death in it and dropped it into the ocean. The box floated a long time in the ocean until it came to Ireland, and was washed on shore. Men got the box up on the shore and began to wonder what was in it. Two big Irishmen got sledge-hammers and broke the box open. Death flew out and killed every man of them. And he started to killin' people all over Ireland. That was why the Irishmen left Ireland and come to America.

82

THE SHEEP ROGUES

A²

There was a hainted house that stood back on a hill. Sheep rogues used to bring their sheep there of a night. The sheep made a lot of noise bleating and running around the place. It scared the man who lived there. He had a nice home and was a wealthy man. He thought that witches were haintin' his house. Finally he got scared to stay there any longer, and he moved off and left the place. It soon growed up with weeds, for no one would stay there. It got scarier-looking than ever.

Finally the man said he'd deed the place to anyone who would go there and stay. Many people went there but they didn't stay. They'd hear the sheep rogues and think they were haints. Of course, the sheep rogues didn't want anyone stayin' there.

At last an old crippled man said he'd go there and stay if he could get there. He was badly crippled up with the rheumatism and couldn't walk a step. Well, one night some man took him over to the house and carried him in. It was dark, and the sheep rogues were prowlin' about. This man carried the old crippled man into the house. Suddenly a figure of a man appeared, and he felt of the crippled man and asked: "Is he fat or lean?" That just about scared the crippled man and the man carrying him to death. The man who was carrying the crippled fellow dropped the poor old man and said: "Take him, damn you, fat or lean. I'm leaving here," and he ran off just as fast as he could, leaving the crippled man there. But the crippled man was scared so bad that he forgot that he was lame. He jumped up and ran so fast that he beat the hounds home.

Of course, when the man come carrying the crippled fellow in, the sheep rogue that was there just thought it was another sheep rogue bringing in another sheep, and he went up and asked the man if he was fat.

B³

In a certain part of the country, there used to be several sheep-thieves. Every night some person in the neighborhood would miss some sheep.

One night three boys started out in search of some lost sheep. They came to the graveyard in the neighborhood, and here the road divided into three directions. They came to the conclusion that one boy should take each of the roads. When they found their sheep they should all meet in the graveyard. The one getting back first was to wait for the others. One boy found his sheep and got back early.

A certain boy in the neighborhood passed by the graveyard and saw this boy sitting on a tombstone and thought he was a ghost. He ran home to tell his cripple father about what he had seen. His father wouldn't believe him until his son carried him to the graveyard. His father hadn't walked for ten years. When they came to the grave where this boy sat with his sheep, the son said to his father, "Now do you see him?" His father said, "No, I don't. You will have to carry me closer." He took him close enough for the boy to see them, and thinking it was one of his friends coming in with a sheep, the boy asked, "Is he fat?" This frightened the boy so much that he dropped his father and ran home as fast as he could. But after all his father beat him home, though he hadn't walked a step in ten years.

NOTES ON CHAPTER VIII

1. Told by the late Frank Schumaker, Grand Tower, who learned it at either first or second hand from an Irish immigrant who had settled in that town and worked at the iron foundry that used to be there.

The theme is a widely used one in European folk tales. Thompson lists numerous variants of it; see his *Motif-Index of Folk Literature*, vol. II, pp. 28–29, D361.1, and vol. IV, p. 403, K1335.

2. Related by Mrs. Mary U. Stallion, Elizabethtown. The story was told as if it were a natural occurrence of the neighborhood. It is not, however, for the region is not devoted to sheep-raising.

3. Secured from Ralph Reynolds, Carterville.

PART II

BALLADS AND SONGS

CHAPTER I

BALLADS AND SONGS

SCHOLARS have long known that Southern Illinois is rich in ballads and songs, but only in recent years have collectors turned their attention to that section. The fertile and picturesque regions of the Appalachian Mountains, of the Ozarks, and of the far West offered them an alluring hunting ground so rich that they have had little time for a less spectacular field. Life in those regions was romantic and quaint, the subject of countless novels and short stories. In the mountains time seemed to have halted two or three centuries ago. Egypt, on the other hand, was only the southern end of Illinois, a hilly and poverty-stricken appendage to a great prairie state. Inhabited as it was by people of Southern descent, it lagged behind the more prosperous regions to the north. It lacks those spectacular qualities that made the mountains appealing; its backwardness was not quaint; its feuds were not romantic, but troublesome instances of lawlessness. Its beauty is not striking enough to tempt strangers to brave the red clay hills in winter and the dusty roads in summer. It has no springs to attract tourists in search of health, and its climate is hot in summer and disagreeable in winter. Transcontinental traffic passes to the north, and the gulf-coast travelers see only thirty miles or so of hills and rocky bluffs, from Carbondale to Dongola. All the rest of the landscape is flat and uninteresting, with collieries rising above the countryside in the northern half of the section. Egypt has only one college, the Southern Illinois State Teachers' College at Carbondale, which until recent times has shown but little interest in folk literature.

Yet Egypt is well worth the attention of collectors of ballads and songs. Although today the custom of ballad-singing is less common than it used to be, it shows a remarkable tenacity, considering the competition of radios and movies. Fortunately, paved roads were somewhat slow to reach Egypt, and certain neighborhoods continued to be isolated during the winter months and thus had to provide their own entertainment. A few years ago one could reach Elizabethtown and Cave-in-Rock in winter only by taking a boat at Golconda or Rosiclare.

Since most Egyptians are descended from settlers who came to Illinois from Kentucky, Tennessee, and North Carolina, songs and ballads current in those states are current in Egypt. Among those brought into this section by the pioneers were English and Scottish ballads included in Child's collection, such as "Barbara Allen" "The Gypsy Laddie," and "Lord Thomas and Fair Annet." Other importations usually of English origin came, too; among them are "Mary o' the Wild Moor" and "The Butcher Boy." A few songs, some of them certainly of American origin, seem to have come from the East. More common, however, are the native American songs and ballads. Among these are such pieces as "Casey Jones," "Johnny Sands," "The Silver Dagger," "Milwaukee Fire," and "The Fatal Wedding." The songs are usually doleful love-songs which follow the convention of crossed love and faithless or murderous bridegrooms. Western songs, such as "Joe Bowers," "Whoopee, Ti Yi Yo," and "The Dying Cowboy," have made their way back to Egypt from the West. Many ballads and songs are concerned with unhappy childhood: for example, songs like "Baggage Coach Ahead," "Page from the Scrap Book of Life," "Song Balet of Birdy," and "The Blind Child." There are, too, a few songs that have been preserved from the temperance movement. Game and nursery songs are fairly common, among which are such pieces as "Poor Robin," "Paper of Pins," "If You Will Marry Me," "Billy Boy," "Weevily Wheat," "Skip to My Lou," and "In the Good Old Colony Days." The last song is one of the earliest that I can remember from my childhood.

In her introduction to *American Ballads and Songs*, Louise Pound observes that ballad-singing "lingers in out-of-the-way places, as in the chimney nook of farm houses, or by the stove in the cross-roads store," that occasionally it is heard in the village and more rarely in the cities. Such is the case in Egypt. In the past the isolation of communities in the foothills of the Ozarks behind miles of hilly red clay roads encouraged ballad-singing, play parties, and square dances. A high degree of illiteracy, an ingrained hostility to change, and a grinding poverty tend to encourage the preservation of the custom to the present day. It is less common now, however, than it was twenty-five or thirty years ago.

Today the collector must hunt for ballad-singers; they are a thinning band, well advanced in years. Seldom do the young people take up their works, for they move to the towns and cities, where they forget the old songs they learned at home. But time has not yet removed the old singers, and occasionally some of the younger generation take up the customs of their fathers. Among a good many country-folk, group-singing is still a lively custom, and in the villages and cities one now and then finds individuals who have written down these songs and ballads in manuscript books. Mrs. Clara Walpert, of Belleville, has preserved a large number of them in manuscript, and she loves to sing them to appreciative audiences. Mrs. Hattie Bitner, of Waltonville, has a collection of songs in manuscript— songs which the young folk of her day sang. Near Carterville the Watsons and the Jameses have a fairly large collection; and it is not difficult to find today, in different sections of Egypt, individuals who sing ballads and songs from memory.

Among the latter a number of people quickly come to mind. My mother, Mrs. Charles Neely, Sr., of Carbondale, still loves to sing ballads and folk-songs that she learned from her cousin, the late Mrs. Nina Crowe. Miss Anna Grommet, of Belleville, remembers a few game-songs. Miss Hallie M. Eubanks, also of Belleville, gave me versions of love-songs that the youth in her neighborhood used to sing. One of the most interesting of these individuals is Fred Kirby of Flora, who was a human fly until he had the misfortune of falling from the Wayne County court-house. He sang several songs and ballads that his mother had taught him. In the last few years this versatile individual constructed a machine with which he played some eight or nine instruments at the same time, making use of his feet, his knees, his hands, and his mouth. The simple music of folk songs and ballads is well adapted to such a machine.

People like the Watsons and Jameses, however, are likely to do more toward preserving the custom of ballad-singing. Gifted with an ear for music, they have trained their children to sing and play folk-songs. They have a string band, which they call the Stringtown Clod Hoppers, made up entirely of Jameses and Watsons. Mr. Matt Watson plays the accordion, Mr. F. F. James the fiddle; one of the James boys and Ivan and Inez Watson play guitars. The band meets weekly or oftener at their homes or at the homes of neighbors to make music. Ivan and Inez usually sing, with a nasal twang, while they play their guitars. Generally they do not begin to sing immediately (they may have been a little shy at my presence) but wait until they have played several pieces. As the evening passes, their enthusiasm seems to rise. Ivan looks over at his sister and they begin to sing some favorite. They are likely to begin with some lively air like "Skip to My Lou."

Then perhaps will follow the lugubrious words of "Drooping Willows."

> "One night in last November,
> When the moon was shining low,
> I went up to her cabin,
> Up to her cabin door,
> Saying, 'Emma, my own true Emma,
> Come let us take a walk,
> Down beneath the drooping willows,
> Our wedding day to talk'. "

Their voices become plaintive as, moved by the tragedy of the song, they relate the cold-blooded slaying of Emma. By the time this song is ended, the whole band seems to be infected by the melancholy air and words and strikes up "Weeping Willow Tree."

> "My heart is broken; I'm in sorrow
> O'er the one I love,
> But I know I'll never see him,
> Till we meet in heaven above.
> Then bury me beneath the weeping tree,
> Beneath the weeping, the weeping willow tree,
> That he may know where I am sleeping
> And perhaps he'll weep for me."

The simple tragedies of the songs are serious and moving to the singers and to the musicians as well. They relive the emotions of the murdered Emma and the grief of the deserted girl. The convention is not trite or conventional to them, but a soul-stirring tragedy.

One does not have to go outside Carbondale to hear folk-music. Not many blocks from the college, Mr. Wright runs a repair-shop, in which he mends anything from a musical instrument to a chair. Promptly at five o'clock each afternoon he lays aside his work and takes up his violin. Usually some guitar-player in the neighborhood joins him, and they play until supper-time.

Most of the airs are breakdowns popular at square dances years ago. One piece follows another in rapid succession until the musicians have had music enough for the day. I have never succeeded in getting words from them. Mr. Wright seems to be a little contemptuous of words; he remembers only music. And of his musical skill he is very proud. He learned his music from an itinerant music-teacher and from correspondence courses, and has given lessons himself. He takes pains to inform one that he can play classical music, too, and to prove his assertion he strikes up some semi-classical number that he plays none too well. He does much better with his breakdowns.

CHAPTER II

BRITISH BALLADS

ENGLISH and Scottish ballads of the Child collection are rather uncommon in Egypt, and those that are current have suffered deterioration at the hands of the transmitters. The ballads have lost many of the details of earlier versions. There is a tendency on the part of the singers to omit the introductory stanzas and to plunge headlong into the climax. And such details as are given sometimes have become sadly disarranged; for instance, in the local variant of "Lord Thomas and Fair Annet," Elender, and not the brown girl, has "house and land." When the singer fails to remember stanzas, he often borrows from some other song or ballad; "The Gypsy Laddie" contains an example of such confusion.

Among Egyptians, English and Scottish ballads do not enjoy the popularity that they appear to have in the Southern Mountains. Perhaps that is to be expected; Egypt has been less protected from outside influences than the mountain regions of Kentucky and Tennessee, less protected than the Ozarks of Arkansas and Missouri. Consequently, in Egypt, British ballads have had to compete with those that concern the American scene, and the native pieces seem to drive out the more exotic foreign ones. Such competition is perhaps less pronounced in the Appalachian and Ozark Mountains than it is in Southern Illinois.

*　　*　　*

I

LORD THOMAS AND FAIR ANNET[1]

This variant of "Lord Thomas and Fair Annet," known locally as "The Brown Girl," proves Miss Pound's contention that the changes which occur in transmission are not always fortunate. "The Brown Girl" has only nine stanzas, less than half of the D Variant of the Child collection. The whole point of the mother's preference for the brown girl is lost, for fair Elender is the one who has house and land. Lord Thomas is not Elender's suitor but her father.

See Francis James Child, *English and Scottish Popular Ballads* (Boston, 1883–1898), no. 73; Louise Pound, *American Ballads and Songs* (New York and Chicago, 1922), no. 12; Phillips Barry, Fannie H. Eckstrom, and Mary W. Smyth, *British Ballads from Maine* (New Haven, 1929), pp. 129–130.

> Oh, Mother, dear Mother, will you discourse,
> Will you discourse as one?
> O, shall I marry fair Elender dear,
> Or bring the Brown girl home?
>
> Fair Elender she has house and land;
> The Brown girl she has none
> Therefore, I charge you with my good blessings
> To bring the Brown girl home.
>
> He rode unto Lord Thomas' dwelling
> And knocked on the ring.
> There was no one there as ready as herself
> To rise and let him in.
>
> "I've news, I've news," said he,
> "I've news to tell to thee.
> I've come to invite you to my wedding today."
> "That's very bad news to me."

He took fair Elender by the hand;
He led her through the hall
And set her down at the head of the table
Among the gentry all.

The Brown girl having a knife in her hand,
And it was long and sharp,
She pierced it under fair Elender's arm,
And pierced it through her heart.

"Fair Elender, dear, and what is the matter?"
"O, can't you very well see;
Oh, can't you see my own heart's blood
A-trickling to my knee?"

He took the Brown girl by the hand
And led her through the hall,
Took down his sword, cut off her head,
And threw it against the wall.

He turned his sword unto his breast,
And on it he did say,
"Here is an end to two true lovers.
God send they're gone to rest."

2

BARBARA ALLEN[2]

"Barbara Allen," on the other hand, seems to have escaped much of the debasing influence of transmission, for it compares fairly well with Child's B Variant, but the Southern Illinois variant was fixed for many years by a broadside, and it has passed through only two hands.

Compare with Child, no. 84; Pound, no. 3; and a variant published in Vance Randolph's *The Ozarks* (New York, 1931), pp. 183-185.

1. In scarlet town where I was born
   There was a fair maid dwelling,
   Made ev'ry youth cry well a-way,
   And her name was Barbara Allen.

2. All in the merry month of May,
   When the green buds were swelling,
   Sweet William came from the Western States
   And courted Barbara Allen.

3. It was all in the month of June,
   When all things they were blooming,
   Sweet William on his death-bed lay
   For the love of Barbara Allen.

4. He sent his servant to the town,
   Where Barbara was a-dwelling,
   "My master is sick and sends for you,
   If your name be Barbara Allen.

5. "And death is painted on his face
   And o'er his heart is stealing;
   Then hasten away to comfort him,
   O lovely Barbara Allen."

6. So slowly, slowly she got up
   And slowly she came nigh him,
   And all she said when she got there,
   "Young man, I think you're dying."

7. "Oh, yes, I'm sick and very sick,
   And death is on me dwelling;
   No better, no better I never can be,
   If I can't have Barbara Allen."

8. "Oh, yes, you're sick and very sick,
   And death is on you dwelling.
   No better, no better you never will be,
   For you can't have Barbara Allen.

9. Oh, don't you remember in yonder town,
   When you were at the tavern,
   You drank the health to the ladies all around
   And slighted Barbara Allen?"

10. As she was on her highway home
    The birds they kept on singing;
    They sang so clear they seemed to say,
    "Hard hearted, Barbara Allen."

11. As she was walking o'er the fields,
    She heard the death bell knelling,
    And every stroke did seem to say,
    "Hard-hearted Barbara Allen."

12. She looked to the east; she looked to the west;
    She spied his corpse a-coming,
    "Lay down, lay down that corpse of clay
    That I may look upon him."

13. The more she looked, the more she mourned,
    Till she fell to the ground a-crying,
    Saying, "Take me up, and take me home,
    For I am now a-dying.

14. "Oh, Mother, oh, Mother, go make my bed;
    Go make it long and narrow;
    Sweet William died for pure, pure love,
    And I shall die for sorrow.

15. "Oh, Father, oh, Father, go dig my grave;
    Go dig it long and narrow;
    Sweet William died for me today;
    I'll die for him tomorrow."

16. She was buried in the old church yard,
    And he was buried a-nigh her;
    On William's grave there grew a red rose,
    On Barbara's grew a green briar.

3

THE GYPSY LADDIE[3]

This ballad is known locally as "Black Jack David;" in some sections of Egypt it is called "Gypsy Davy." This variant has deteriorated sadly. Only three stanzas, changed considerably from the Child versions, remain. It has been confused, moreover, with "Weevily Wheat;" stanzas 3 and 4 are perhaps taken from a variant of this song current in the neighborhood from which "Black Jack David" came.[4]

For comparison see Child, no. 200, and Barry, Ekcstrom, Smyth, pp. 269–272.

Black Jack David came riding down the lane,
Singing so loud and gaily,
Making all the woods round him ring
To charm the heart of a lady.
To charm the heart of a lady.

"How old are you, my pretty little miss?
How old are you, my honey?"
She answered me with a smile and kiss,
"I'll be seventeen next Sunday.
I'll be seventeen next Sunday."

"Will you go with me, my pretty little miss?
Will you go with me, my honey?"
She answered me with a smile and kiss,
"I'll go with you next Sunday.
I'll go with you next Sunday."

She pulled off her low heel shoes,
All made of Spanish leather.
She put on her high heel shoes,
And they rode off together,
And they rode off together.

Last night she slept on a warm feather bed
Beside her husband and baby.
Tonight she sleeps on the cold, cold ground
By the side of Black Jack David,
By the side of Black Jack David.

4

WILLIAM AND MARGARET[5]

This ballad is really a variant of "Margaret's Ghost,"[6] written by David Mallet and published in Percy's *Reliques of Ancient English Poetry*. It must have been learned originally from Percy's *Reliques* or from some volume which reprinted Mallet's ballad. Although less than half of "Margaret's Ghost" remains, one is forced to the conclusion that the ballad was transmitted by people with remarkable memories, or that it has not long been a part of oral tradition. The latter seems more likely. In the first place, those stanzas omitted are not vital to the narrative, being usually descriptive or conversational. In the second place, only two complete lines have been substituted and six words in other lines; only one word has been left out and one phrase rearranged.

See Percy's *Reliques of Ancient English Poetry*, Vol. III, Book iii, no. 16 (pp. 308–311) in the ed. by Henry Wheatley (London, 1891).

'Twas At the Silent Midnight Hour

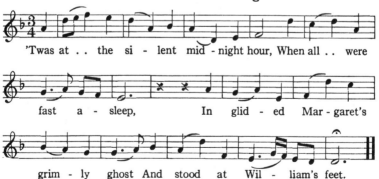

'Twas at . . the si - lent mid - night hour, When all . . were

fast a - sleep, In glid - ed Mar - garet's

grim - ly ghost And stood at Wil - liam's feet.

1. 'Twas at the silent midnight hour
   When all were fast asleep;
   In glided Margaret's grimly ghost,
   And stood at William's feet.

2. Her face was like an April morn,
   Clad in wintry cloud,
   And clay cold was her lily hand
   That held was sable shroud.

3. "Awake," she cried, "thy true love calls,
   Come from her midnight grave;
   Now let thy pity hear the maid,
   Thy love refused to save.

4. "Why did you promise love to me,
   And not thy promise keep?
   Why did you swear my eyes were bright
   Yet leave those eyes to weep?

5. "How could you say my face was fair,
   And yet that face forsake?
   How could you win my virgin heart
   Yet leave that heart to break?"

6. The lark sung loud, the morning smiled
   And raised her glittering head
   Pale William quaked in every limb,
   And raving left his bed.

7. He hied him to the fatal place
   Where Margaret's body lay,
   And stretched him on the green grass turf
   That wrapt her breathless clay.

8. And thrice he called on Margaret's name,
   And thrice he wept full sore,
   Then laid his cheek to the cold grave,
   And word spake never more.

NOTES ON CHAPTER II

1. Secured from Mr. William H. Creed, Belleville, who got it from a manuscript book belonging to Mrs. Clara Walpert, also of Belleville.

2. Miss Emilie Huck, New Baden, gave me this variant, which she had obtained from Miss Catherine Kettler of New Baden. Miss Kettler learned it from an old broadside, which had been in the family for two or three generations.

3. Obtained from Mr. Frank Irvin, Mascoutah. This variant of "The Gypsy Laddie" was one of the songs that the young people used to sing in the evening at Broughton. Child's B Variant is a little like "Black Jack David," and Barry, Eckstrom, Smyth's Variant B has two stanzas that are very much like two in the Southern Illinois variant—stanzas 1 and 8, which go thus:

> "The Gypsy Davy came over the hills,
> Came over the eastern valley,
> He sang till he made the green woods ring,
> And charmed the heart of a lady.
>
> . . . .
>
> Last night I slept in a warm, soft bed,
> And in my arms my baby,
> To-night I'll lie on the cold, cold ground,
> Beside of Gypsy Davy."

4. "Weevily Wheat" is current in a number of variants in Southern Illinois; see pp. 212–213. John Lomax has a variant of the song (*American Ballads and Folk Songs* (New York, 1934), pp. 292–293) with a stanza somewhat like the third stanza of "Black Jack David."

> "How old are you, my pretty little Miss?
> How old are you, my honey?
> She answered me with a 'Ha, ha' laugh,
> 'I'll be sixteen next Sunday.' "

One can see how the confusion might have happened when one remembers that Child's B Variant contains a stanza (Number 4) which begins

> " 'Will you go with me, my hinny and my heart?
> Will you go with me, my dearie?' "

5. Secured from Miss Esther Knefelkamp, Belleville, who got both the words and the music from Miss Amelia Zehner of Belleville.

6. Nine of the seventeen stanzas of "Margaret's Ghost" published in Percy's *Reliques* have been omitted from the Southern Illinois variant: three stanzas between Stanzas 2 and 3, two between 3 and 4, and four between 5 and 6. Of the remaining stanzas the following changes have occurred in the later variant:

Stanza 1
    line 1 "midnight" for "solemn"
    line 2 "When all were fast asleep" for
        "When night and morning meet" (entire line)

Stanza 2
    line 2 "A" omitted between "in" and "wintry"
    line 4 "fable" for "sable"

Stanza 4
    line 2 "thy" for "that"

Stanza 6
>   line 2 "And raised her glittering head" for
>   "With beams of rosy red" (entire line)
>   line 3 "quaked" for "shook" and "every" for "ev'ry"

Stanza 7
>   line 3 "green grass turf" for "grass-green turf"

Stanza 8
>   line 3 "the" for "her."

CHAPTER III

OTHER IMPORTED BALLADS

THE BALLADS included in this chapter are of foreign origin — possibly British.[1] In Egypt they appear to enjoy a greater popularity than the traditional Scottish and English ballads collected by Professor Child. This popularity may result from the fact that they are more in keeping with the tone and spirit of American ballads and songs than the Child ballads are. The tragedies narrated might have had American settings, and the actors might have been American men and women. They are ballads of singers who have lost the artless high seriousness, the simple dignity, and the unstudied charm of the traditional English and Scottish pieces.

*   *   *

5

THE BUTCHER BOY

This is a very popular ballad in Southern Illinois, current in numerous variants. The scene of the ballad is likely to shift with the singers; sometimes it is Jersey City, sometimes Jefferson City, and sometimes New York City. Simple as this story is, the details vary from singer to singer; in one variant, for example, it is the butcher boy who commits suicide.

See Pound, no. 24; John H. Cox, *Folk-Songs of the South* (Cambridge [Mass.], 1925), no. 145; William Roy Mackenzie, *Ballads and Sea Songs from Nova Scotia* (Cambridge [Mass.], 1928), no. 59.

Butcher Boy

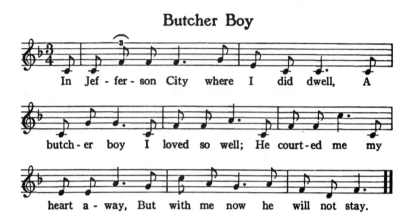

In Jef-fer-son City where I did dwell, A butch-er boy I loved so well; He court-ed me my heart a-way, But with me now he will not stay.

A²

In Jefferson City where I did dwell,
A butcher boy I loved so well;
He courted me my heart away,
But with me now he will not stay.

Oh, grieve, oh grieve, oh tell me why,
Because he had more gold than I;
But gold will melt and silver fly;
Then he will be as poor as I.

She went upstairs; the bed she made
And not a word to her mother she said.
"Oh, what's the matter, Daughter dear?"
"It's not to tell you, Mother dear."

She took a chair and set me down.
"With pen and ink I'll write it down."
In every line she dropped a tear;
In every verse was "Willie dear."

Her father came home from work that night
And asking for his daughter dear,
He went upstairs; the door he broke
And found her hanging on a rope.

He took his knife and cut her down,
And on her bosom this note was found;

.   .   .   .

.   .   .   .

"Go dig my grave both wide and deep;
Place marble stones from head to feet
And on my stone a turtle dove,
To show the world that I died for love."

B³

In Jersey City where I did dwell,
A butcher boy I loved so well
Once courted me both night and day,
And now with me he will not stay.

There stands a home in yonder town;
There goes my love and sits him down;
He takes a strange girl on his knee
And tells her what he once told me.

The reason is I'll tell you why,
Because she has more gold than I,
But gold will melt and silver fly,
And she will be as poor as I.

There sits a bird in yonder tree;
They say he's blind and cannot see;
I wish it had been the same with me
Before he sought my company.

Go dig my grave both wide and deep,
Place a tombstone at my head and feet,
Place on my breast a snow white dove
That the world may know I died for love.

And when her father he came home,
He said, "Where has my daughter gone?"
He went up stairs; the door he broke
And found her hanging by a rope.

He took a knife and cut her down,
And on her breast these words he found;
"Oh, foolish, foolish, wasn't I,
To hang myself for a butcher b'y?"

C⁴

In Jersey City where I did dwell
A butcher boy I loved so well;
He courted me my heart away,
And now with me he will not stay.

There is another girl in this same town;
My love he goes and sits him down;
He takes the strange girl on his knee
And tells her what he don't tell me.

It is a grief to me, and I'll tell you why
Because she has more gold than I,
But her gold will melt and silver fly,
And in time of need she be poor as I.

Oh, what a foolish maid am I
To hang myself for a butcher boy.
Go dig my grave both wide and deep;
Place a marble stone at my head and feet
And on my breast a turtle dove
To show the world I died for love.

D⁵

In Jefferson City where I did dwell,
A butcher boy I loved so well,
He courted me my heart away,
But with me now he will not stay.

O grieve, oh grieve, o tell me why,
Because he had more loves than I.

.   .   .   .

.   .   .   .

. . . .
I found him hanging by a rope;
I took my knife and cut him down
And in his bosom this note I found:

"Go dig my grave both wide and deep;
Place maul (sic) stone from head to feet
And on my grave a turtle dove,
To show the world I died for love."

6

MARY O' THE WILD MOOR[6]

See Pound, no. 35, Cox, *Folk-Songs of the South*, no.
148, and Mackenzie, no. 61.

It was a cold winter night,
And the moon pale bright shone o'er hill and vale.
Poor Mary came wandering home with her babe
Till she came to her own father's door.

"Oh, Father, dear Father," she cried,
"Come down and open the door,
Or the child in my arms will perish and die
By the wind that blows across the wild moor."

The old man was deaf to her cry;
Not a sound of her voice reached his ear,
But the watch dog howled and the village bell tolled,
And the wind blew across the wild moor.

But how must the man have felt,
When he came to the door in the morn?
Poor Mary was dead, but the child was alive,
Closely pressed in its dead mother's arms.

The old man in grief pined away,
And the child to its mother went soon,
And no one, they say, has lived there to this day,
And the cottage to ruin has gone.

7

THE WAXFORD GIRL[7]

This ballad is a local variant of "The Wexford Girl" with most of the story lost. Belden (*Journal of American Folklore* XXV, p. 11) believes that the song is based upon "The Berkshire Tragedy, or, the Wittam Miller," an eighteenth-century broadside ballad. Mackenzie (*Ballads and Sea Songs from Nova Scotia*, p. 293) says that it is found in oral circulation in Virginia, Tennessee, Kentucky, Mississippi, and Missouri.

The first and second stanzas are somewhat like Stanzas 8 and 9 of the ballad as given by Mackenzie in his *Ballads and Sea Songs from Nova Scotia*.

"My son, my son, what have you done
To bloody your hands and clothes?"
The answer that he gave her
Was the bleeding of the nose.

He asked her for a candle
To light him to his bed;
And then that night while sleeping
This maid ran through his head.

He took her by the locks of hair,
As we may understand,
And throwed her in the river
Just below the old mill dam.

"Lye there, lye there, you Waxford girl;
You thought you would be my bride,
But never shall you be my bride
Or unto me be tied."

8

THE OLD WOMAN FROM SLAB CITY[8]

Cox (*Folk-Songs of the South*, no. 157, p. 464) includes a variant of this ballad under the title, "An Old Woman's Story," which is somewhat like the Southern Illinois variant. In Scotland, he says, the ballad is known as "The Wife of Kelso" or "The Wily Auld Carle." Although very similar to "Johnny Sands," this is a different piece.

> There was an old woman in Slab City;
> In Slab City she did dwell
> She lovéd her old man dearly
> But another one twice as well.
> Sing tither the ann the aye rē-ā;
> Sing tither the an rē-ā.
>
> She mixed up some nerve and bone
> And made him drink it all.
> Says he, "My dear and loving wife
> I can't see you at all."
> Says he, "I can't see you at all;
> I can't see you at all."
>
> Says he, "I'll go and drown myself
> If I could find the way."
> Says she, "I'll go along with you,
> For fear you go astray."
> Sing tither the ann the aye rē-ā;
> Sing tither the an rē-ā.
>
> They walked along; they trudged along,
> Till they came to the river shore.
> Says he, "My dear and loving wife,
> You'll have to push me o'er."
> Sing tither the ann the aye rē-ā;
> Sing tither the an rē-ā.

She stepped back a step or two,
To run and push him in.
He being nimble stepped aside,
And she fell headlong in.
Sing tither the ann the aye rē-ā;
Sing tither the an rē-ā.

And finding out her sad mistake,
She began to scream and bawl.
Says he, "My dear and loving wife,
I can't see you at all."
Says he, "I can't see you at all;
I can't see you at all."

He being of good nature
And fearing she might swim,
He got himself a great long pole
And pushed her farther in.
Sing tither the ann the aye rē-ā;
Sing tither the an rē-ā.

And now my song is ended,
And I can't sing any more,
But wasn't she a great big fool,
She didn't swim ashore!

9

PRETTY BETSEY THE MILKMAID[9]

This ballad was brought from Stratfordshire, England, three generations ago. Apparently, it is not widely known. It seems rather to be the property of one family. The heroine of this song suggests Pamela, for like her Pretty Betsey is rewarded for her virtue.

A squire and his sister
They sat in a hall.
As they were singing
Some sad, mournful song,
Pretty Betsey, the milkmaid,
Came tripping along.

"Do you want any new milk?"
Pretty Betsey she said.
"Oh, yes," said young squire,
"Step ye in, pretty maid
And set ye down by me,
And my bride I will make you,
And soon it shall be."

"Oh, it's hold your tongue, squire,
And let me go free,
And don't make such game
Of my sad poverty.
There are ladies passing
More fitting than me.

"I am just a poor milkmaid
Brought up on a cow."
The ring from his finger
He gave it thereon,
And straight through the middle
He broke it in two.

One half he gave to Betsey,
As I have been told;
So they both went a-walking
Down the blackberry fold.
The squire said to Betsey,
"Let me have my will

"And constant remaining
With your fair body,
And if you deny me
In this wide open field,
Oh, my dear, I will force you
Against your own will."

With huggling and struggling
Pretty Betsey got free,
And with her sharp scissors
She pierced his body.
She pierced his fair body
Till the blood did flow;
Straight to her master
Like lightning did go.

Straight home to her master
With tears in her eyes,
"I've wounded your young squire;
In danger he lies.
It was on my fair body
He began to prove bold;
So I left him bleeding
Down blackberry fold."

The cab was sent for,
And the squire brought home
And also two doctors
To heal up his wounds.
His wounds were healed
And as always cured.

So they sent for pretty Betsey,
The charming milkmaid.
The parson was sent for
And this couple joined,
And soon they enjoyed
Their new married life.

About six years after
The young squire died
And left me two babies
To lie by my side.
So it's better to be honest,
If you're ever so poor.
So he made me his lady
Because I was poor.

10

THE SOLDIER'S FAREWELL[10]

This song and the one which follows came directly
from Scotland and are probably known only in limited
circles in Belleville.

On the banks of Clyde stood a lad and a lassie.
The lad's name wis Geordie; the lassie's wis Jean.
She flung her airms roon him and cried, "Dinna leave
    me,"
For Georgie wis going to fight for his Queen.

chorus:

Over the burning plains of Egypt, under the scorching
    sun,
He thought of the stories he would have to tell his love
    when the fight was won,
And he treasured with care the dear lock of hair,
But his darling, dear Jeanie, she prayed,
But her prayers were in vain, for she'll never see again
Her lad in the Scotch brigade.

She gave him a lock of her dear golden tresses;
He kissed her and pressed her
Once more to his breast till his eyes spoke
Of love, which his lips could not utter.

11

WHAT WILL YE BRING TAE ME?[11]

Lassie sings:

When ye gang awa', Jamie, far across the sea, laddie,
An' when ye gand tae Germany what will ye bring tae
me, laddie?

Laddie sings:

I'll bring ye a braw new gown, lassie,
I'll bring ye a braw new gown, lassie,
An' it will be o'gowden grey with Valences a roon, lassie.

NOTES TO CHAPTER III

1. Louise Pound (*American Ballads and Songs*) includes "The Butcher Boy" and "Mary o'the Wild Moor" in her chapter entitled "Other Imported Ballads" and Songs." Cox (*Folk-Songs of the South*, p. 430) says that "The Butcher Boy" has resulted from a fusion of extracts from "Sheffield Pork," "The Squire's Daughter" (also known as "The Cruel Father, or, Deceived Maid"), and "A Brisk Young Sailor" (called in an abbreviated variant "There is an Alehouse in Yonder Town"). Mackenzie (*Ballads and Sea Songs from Nova Scotia*, p. 157) expresses the same conclusion. He likewise remarks (*ibid.*, p. 164) that "Mary o'the Wild Moor" exists in numerous English Broadsides.

2. Obtained from Miss Irene Mache, Belleville. She learned it from Mrs. Henrietta Knefelkamp, also of that city, who learned the song from a neighbor. Pound, no. 24; Cox, no. 145; Mackenzie, no. 59.

3. Mr. Dave H. Adamson, Belleville, gave me this variant, which he had secured from a student in the public school of that city.

4. Secured by Mr. William H. Creed, Belleville, from the manuscript book of Mrs. Clara Walpert of that city.

5. Miss Irene Mache also gave me this variant, which she obtained from Mrs. Ida Thorman, Belleville.

6. Obtained from Miss Emilie Huck, New Baden, Illinois, who secured it from Miss Ruth Ellen Asbury of New Baden. Miss Asbury learned it from her grandmother, Mrs. Ella Smith, who memorized the song when she was a girl.

7. Communicated by Mr. William H. Creed, Belleville, who got it from the manuscript book of Mrs. Clara Walpert, of Belleville. Mackenzie, no. 115.

8. Miss Helen Piper, Oakdale, gave me this ballad, which she learned from her father.

9. Secured by Mr. Dave H. Adamson, Belleville, who obtained it from Mrs. Earl Stoeckel, of Belleville; Mrs. Stoeckel learned it from her mother, Mrs. Mary Boden, who learned it from her mother, Mrs. Mary Babering. Mrs. Babering brought the piece from Stratfordshire, England, when she came to this country.

10. Obtained from Miss Anna Grommet, Belleville, who got it from Mr. Alexander Scrobbie, of Belleville. He brought it from Hamilton, Lanarkshire, Scotland.

11. Secured by Miss Anna Grommet from Mr. Alexander Scrobbie.

CHAPTER IV

AMERICAN BALLADS

BALLADS included in this chapter, with few exceptions, are of American origin. Those of foreign ancestry have been so completely revised and altered that they readily pass for native pieces. Only the ballad scholar will recognize them as importations.

In subject-matter these ballads cling closely to ballad conventions; they deal with murderous lovers, faithful love, thwarted love, faithless husbands, spectacular tragedies, and, in a lighter vein, with a termagant wife and a fickle girl. They find poetry in railway wrecks and tragic fires; often the treatment seems a bit facile for such calamitous subjects. Humor in the two ballads of a jovial nature is broad, springing in the one instance from the turning of the tables on a shrewish woman and in the other from a purse-proud father's finding himself bested by the sentimental vagaries of his daughter.

Several of these ballads have a fairly wide circulation in Southern Illinois, in variants that differ to a considerable extent in text. With one exception the variants come from sections relatively distant from one another.

12

PEARL BRYANT

Two variants of this ballad are known in Egypt, the second one under the title, "Drooping Willows." The usual name of the piece seems to be "The Jealous Lover" or "Pearl Bryan."

Cox (*Folk-Songs of the South*, no. 38) quotes a letter from Mr. Clifford R. Meyers, State Historian and Archivist of West Virginia, which explains why the ballad sometimes has the title, "Pearl Bryan." According to Mr. Meyers, a girl of that name, residing in Greencastle, Indiana, was murdered January 31, 1896, as a result of a criminal operation performed by two young doctors or dental students, Scott Jackson and Alonzo Walling. The girl's body was found near Fort Thomas, Kentucky. This variant of the ballad made its way into Tennessee and then into Pope County, Illinois. Somewhere along the route Bryan became Bryant. (Note the similarities between this and *The Daemon Lover* [Child no. 243]—J. W. A.)

Pearl Bryant

A[1]

Deep, deep in yonder valley
Where the violets fade and bloom
There lies my own Pearl Bryant
In the cold and silent tomb.
She died not broken-hearted,
Nor lingering sickness fell,
But in an instant parted
From a home she loved so well.

One evening the moon shone brightly,
And the stars were shining, too.
Up to her cottage window
Her jealous lover drew.
"Come, Pearl, let's take a ramble
O'er the meadows deep and gay.
There, no one can disturb us,
And we'll name our wedding day."

Deep, deep into the valley
He led his love so dear.
Says she, "It's for you only
That I am rambling here.
The way seems dark and dreary,
And I'm afraid to stay;
Of rambling I've grown weary
And would retrace my way."

"Retrace your way you'll never;
These woods you'll never more roam.
So bid farewell for ever
To parents, friends, and home.
From me you cannot hide;
No human arm can save you;
Pearl Bryant, you must die."

Down on her knees before him
She pleaded for her life,
But deep into her bosom
He plunged a fatal knife.
"What have I done, Scott Jackson,
For you to take my life?
You know that I have always loved you
And would have been your wife.

Good-bye, dear loving parents;
I'll never see you more,
Tho' long you'll wait my coming
At the little cottage door.
But I will forgive you, Jackson."
Those where her dying words.
Her pulse had ceased their beating
And her eyes were closed in death.

The birds sang in the morning
Their awful, weary song.
They found Pearl Bryant lying
Upon the cold, cold ground.
She died not broken-hearted,
Nor lingering sickness fell,
But in an instant parted
From a home she loved so well.

B²

This variant is known as "Drooping Willows." Cox
(*Folk-Songs of the South*, no. 38) prints variants under
titles "Blue-Eyed Ella" (B) and "The Jealous Lover"
(G) respectively, in which the name of the girl is Ella
and that of the murderer is Edward.

One night in last November,
When the moon was shining low,
I went up to her cabin,
Up to her cabin door,

Saying, "Emma, my own true Emma,
Come let us take a walk
Down beneath the drooping willows
Our wedding day to talk."

The night grew dark and gloomy,
And Emma was afraid to stay.
"Oh, Edward, I must leave you.
Oh, Edward, I cannot stay."

"No, Emma, my own true Emma,
From thee I never will part;
I would take this silver dagger;
I would pierce it through your heart."

Down, down she knelt beside him,
Dearly begging for her life;
Into her snowy white bosom
He pierced the silver knife.

"Oh, Edward, I will forgive you."
This was her last sweet sigh;
Down beneath those willows
He left her there to die.

Beneath those drooping willows
Where the early violets bloom,
There sleeps the fair young Emma
In a cold and silent tomb.

She died not broken-hearted,
Neither sickness caused her death;
It was a jealous lover
That took away her breath.

Don't get jealous, dear girls;
Don't get jealous, dear boys;
For jealousy only brings you sorrow
And takes away the joys.

13

THE SILVER DAGGER[3]
TO ALL TRUE LOVERS WHOM
PARENTS WILL PART

This is a somewhat debased variant, in which most
of the poetry has been lost in transmission. Pound,
no. 52, gives two variants and Cox, no. 109, gives three.

All except the last variant of Cox's, called "The Warning Death," have the title, "The Silver Dagger."

> Come men and women, pay good attention
> To what few lines I'll soon relate.
> They are as true as ever was mentioned
> About a young and beautiful bride.
>
> Once there was a young man; he courted a lady.
> He loved her as he loved his life;
> He vowed to her, to her forever
> To be his lawful happy wife.
>
> And when his parents came to know this,
> They strive to part them night and day,
> Saying, "Son, oh son, oh don't you have her,
> For she is a poor girl and it is often said."
>
> And when this lady came to know this,
> She wandered up and through the city.
> She wandered down to Chirfone River
> His rosy cheeks to view no more.
>
> She then took out her silver dagger
> And pierced it through her own white breast.
> It's first she reeled and then she staggered,
> Crying, "Oh, my dear, I'm going to rest."
>
> He being near, he heard her crying
> And knew too well the fainting voice.
> He ran up like some one distracted,
> Crying, "Oh, my dear! I fear you're lost."
>
> He then picked up the silver dagger
> And pierced it through his own brave heart,
> Saying, "Let this be a good rewarding
> For all true lovers that parents will part."

14

THE FATAL WEDDING[4]

For textual comparison see Pound, no. 63.

The wedding bells were ringing
On a moonlight winter night;
The church was decorated;
All within was gay and bright.
A mother with her baby
Came and saw those lights aglow;
She thought of how those same bells
Chimed for her three years ago.

Chorus:

While the wedding bells were ringing,
While the bride and groom were there,
Marching up the aisle together
As the organ pealed an air,
Telling tales of fond affections,
Vowing never more to part,
Just another fatal wedding,
Just another broken heart.

"I'd like to be admitted, sir,"
She begged the sexton old,
"Just for the sake of the baby,
To protect him from the cold."
But he told her that the wedding
Was for the rich and grand;
With this eager, watching crowd
Outside she'd have to stand.

She begged the sexton just once more
To let her step inside;
"For baby's sake you may come in."
The gray-haired man replied.
"If anyone knows the reason
Why this couple should not wed,
Speak now or else forever
Hold your peace," the preacher said.

"I must object," a woman cried,
Her voice so weak and mild;
"The bridegroom is my husband, sir,
And this (his) little child."
"What proof have you?" the preacher asked.
"My baby, sir," she cried,
And knelt to pray to God in heaven;
The little one had died.

The parents of the bride
Then took the outcast by the arm;
"We'll care for you through life," they said;
"You've saved our child from harm."
The parents, bride, and outcast wife
In a carriage rolled away;
The bridegroom died by his own side
Before the break of day.

No wedding feast was spread that night;
Two graves were made next day;
In one the little baby
And in one the father laid.
The story has been often told
By firesides warm and bright
Of bride and groom and outcast wife
On that fatal wedding night.

15

BAD COMPANIONS[5]

Lomax (*Cowboy Songs* (New York, 1910), pp. 81–82)
published a variant of this ballad under the title "Young
Companions." The Southern Illinois variant has one
less stanza than the Lomax version; the third stanza
of his variant is lacking in the one from Egypt. This
stanza goes thus:

"I did not like my fireside,
I did not like my home;
I had in view far rambling,
So far away did roam."

. . . .

Come, all you young companions,
And listen unto me;
I'll tell you a sad story
Of some bad company.

I came from Pennsylvania,
Was born among the hills,
And memories of my childhood
Are warm within me still.

I had a kind old mother,
Who often plead with me;
In her last words at parting
She prayed to God for me.

I had a loving sister
As kind as one could be,
And down on knees before me
She prayed and wept for me.

I bade adieu to loved ones;
To home I bade farewell,
And landed in Chicago
In the very depths of hell.

'Twas there I took to drinking;
I sinned both night and day,
And yet within my bosom
A trembling voice would say:

"Oh, fare thee well my loved one!
May God protect my boy.
I gladly would go with him;
To guide him would be joy."

I courted a fair maiden;
Her name I will not tell,
For I would not disgrace her
As I am doomed for hell.

'Twas a moonlight evening
While the stars were shining bright
That with a golden dagger
I gave her spirit flight.

Then justice overtook me;
You all can plainly see;
My soul is doomed to torture
Throughout eternity.

'Tis now I'm on the scaffold;
My moments are not long;
You may forget the singer,
But don't forget the song.

16

MILWAUKEE FIRE[6]

See Pound no. 62. The Southern Illinois variant is
somewhat abbreviated.

'Twas the gray of early morning when the dreadful cry
    of fire
Rang out upon the cold and piercing air.
Just that little word alone was all it did require
For to spread dismay and panic everywhere.

Milwaukee was excited as it never was before
And learning that the fire bells all around
Were ringing to eternity one hundred souls or more,
And the new Hall House was burning to the ground.

Chorus:

Oh, hear the fire bells ringing on the morning's early
dawn.
Hear those voices as they gave the dreadful cry.
Hear their wail of terror, hear them loudly say,
"Help to protect them, for they are waiting there to
die."

When that dreadful cry was sounded through that
oft condemned hotel
They rushed in mad confusion every way.
The smoke was suffocating and blinding them as well,
And the Fire King could not be held at bay.

From every open window men and woman would
beseech
For help in tones of anguish and despair.
What must have been their feelings when the ladders
would not reach,
And they felt death grasping 'round them everywhere!

The firemen worked like demons and did all within
their power
To save a life or try to soothe the pain,
But all to no avail, for in less than half an hour
All was hushed and further efforts were in vain.

17

CASEY JONES

"Casey Jones" is a popular ballad in Southern Illinois,
as it is in many other sections of the nation. One can
easily secure a dozen or more variants. Pound printed
one variant, *Ballads*, no. 59; Carl Sandburg one, *The
American Songbag* (New York, 1927), pp. 367–368;

Lomax one, *American Ballads and Folk Songs*, pp. 36–
39. None of these is exactly like these two Southern
Illinois variants.

A⁷

Come, all you rounders, if you want to hear
A story about a brave engineer;
Casey Jones was the rounder's name,
On a six eight-wheeler he won his fame.

The caller called Casey at a half-past four.
Kissed his wife at the station door,
Mounted to the cabin with his orders in his hand,
And he took his farewell trip to that promised land.

Chorus

Casey Jones mounted to the cabin,
Casey Jones with his orders in his hand;
Casey Jones mounted to the cabin
And he took his farewell trip to that promised land.

Put in your water and shovel in your coal.
Put your head out the window, watch them drivers
    roll;
I'll run her till she leaves the rail
'Cause I'm eight hours late with that Western mail.

He looked at his watch and his watch was slow;
He looked at the water and the water was low;
He turned to the fireman, and he said;
"We're going to reach 'Frisco, but we'll all be dead."

Chorus

Casey Jones going to reach 'Frisco,
Casey Jones, but we'll all be dead;
Casey Jones, going to reach 'Frisco,
We're going to reach 'Frisco, but we'll all be dead.

Casey pulled up that Reno Hill;
He tooted for the crossing with an awful shrill;
The switchmen knew by the engine's moan
That the man at the throttle was Casey Jones.

He pulled up within two miles of the place,
Number four stared him right in the face;
Turned to the fireman, said: "Boy, you'd better
    jump,
'Cause there's two locomotives that's a-going to
    bump."
Chorus

Casey Jones, two locomotives,
Casey Jones, that's a-going to bump;
Casey Jones, two locomotives,
There's two locomotives that's a-going to bump.

Casey said just before he died,
"There's two more roads that I'd like to ride."
Fireman said, "What could be?"
"The Southern Pacific and the Santa Fe!"

Mrs. Jones sat on her bed a-sighing.
Just received a message that Casey was dying.
Said: "Go to bed, children, and hush your crying,
'Cause you got another papa on the Salt Lake Line."

Chorus

Casey Jones, got another papa,
Mrs. Casey Jones, on that Salt Lake Line,
Casey Jones, got another papa,
You got another papa on the Salt Lake Line.

B[8]

Come, all you rounders, I want you to hear
The story of a brave engineer;
Casey Jones was the rounder's name
On a big eight-wheeler of a mighty fame.

Chorus:

Casey Jones, he pushed on the throttler;
Casey Jones was a brave engineer;
Come on, Casey, and blow the whistler,
Blow the whistles so they all can hear.

Now, Casey said, "Before I die
There's one more trail that I want to try,
And I will try ere many a day
The Union Pacific and the Santa Fe."

Caller called Casey about half-past four;
He kissed his wife at the station door,
Climbed in his cab and was on his way,
"I've got my chance on the Santa Fe."

Down the slope he went on the fly
Heard the fireman say, "You got a white eye."
Well the switchman knew by the engine's moan
That the man at the throttle was Casey Jones.

The rain was a-pounding down like lead;
The railroad track was a river bed;
They slowed her down to a thirty-mile gait,
And the south-bound mail was eight hours late.

Fireman says, "Casey you're running too fast,
You run the black board the last station you
　　passed."
Casey says, "I believe we'll make it through.
For the steam's much better than I ever knew."

Around the curve comes a passenger train,
Her headlight was shining in his eyes through the rain;
Casey blew the whistles a mighty blast,
But the locomotive was a-coming fast.

The locomotives met in the middle of the hill,
In a head-on tangle that's bound to kill;
He tried to do his duty, the yard men said,
But Casey Jones was scalded dead.

Headaches and heartaches and all kinds of pain,
They all ride along with the railroad train,
Stories of brave men, noble and grand,
Belong to the life of the railroad man.

18

ENGINE BELLS[9]

This ballad is apparently not very well known. One
suspects that it was composed by some local poetaster
who was inspired by a railroad tragedy.

'Twas on the evening of the twelfth;
The hour was half past seven;
The sun's bright rays had scarcely lost
Its brightness in the heaven.

The New York Express came up the track
In a lightning rate of speed;
A husband and his loving wife
Unconscious drove their steed.

Chorus:
To hear those engin (sic) bells
The whistel perced (sic) the air;
The dangerous signal came too late
A presious (sic) life to spair.

They drove ahead; no thoughts of death
Would ever accor to them,
But when too late they saw their fate
And was struck by number ten.

The engin stopped; the train backed up;
They all came from their seats,
And as they gased on that sad seen
It caused strong hearts to weep.

It caused a moment of dispear;
The life of one was o'er;
A loving wife lay cold in death,
A husband near death's door.

An angel's face looked down on them
In the moonlight cold and pale;
A smashed-up buggy and a horse
And the engin told the tale.

19

DEATH OF GARFIELD[10]

See Pound, no. 65, for a complete text of the ballad.
One stanza, possibly the chorus, was all that I could
get. It is practically the same stanza that my mother
sings.

My name is Charles J. Guitteau
My name I never deny
For the murder of James Garfield
On the scaffold I must die.

20

THE PRETTY MOHEA

Kittredge expresses the opinion that "The Pretty
Mohea" is a chastened American revision of "The
Indian Lass" known in English broadsides. Frank Kid-
son (*Traditional Tunes*, Oxford, 1891, pp. 110–111) has
printed a version of "The Indian Lass." See *Journal of
American Folklore*, XXXV, 408 and *Harper's Monthly
Magazine*, May, 1915, CXXX, p. 906. Cox (*Folk-Songs
of the South*, no. 116) published three variants; Pound
(*Ballads*, no. 91) one variant; Mackenzie (*Ballads and*

Sea Songs from Nova Scotia, no. 58) one variant; Lomax (*American Ballads and Folk Songs,* pp. 163–165) one variant; Harvey Henry Fuson (*Ballads of the Kentucky Highlands,* London, 1931, p. 84) one variant.

A[11]

This variant is known by the title, "The Little Mohee," which is also the title of the Lomax variant.

As I was out walking for pleasure one day,
The sweet recreation I scarcely can say.
As I sat amusing myself on the grass,
Who should draw near me but a fair Indian Lass?

She sat down beside (me), taking hold of my hand,
Saying, "You are a stranger and in a strange land.
But if you will follow, you're welcome to come
And share with Mohee in what she calls home."

The sun was fast sinking far over the sea
As I wandered along with my little Mohee.
She asked me to marry and offered her hand,
Saying, "My father's the chieftain all over this land."

"Oh, no, my fair maiden, that never could be,
For I have a true love in my own country.
I will not forsake her, for I know she loves me;
Her love is as true as the little Mohee."

'Twas early one morning, one morning in May
I went to this fair maiden; these words I did say:
"I'm going to leave you; so fare-thee-well, dear;
My ship sails are spreading, and home I must steer."

The last time I saw her she stood on the sand,
And as I passed by her she waved her small hand,
Saying, "When you get back to the one you love,
Remember the Mohee in the cocoanut grove."

And now I have got back to my own native shore;
My friends and relations gather around me once
　　more.
I stood and looked around me; no one could I see
That I could compare with the little Mohee.

The girl that I loved proved untrue to me;
So I'll turn my course backward far over the sea.
I'll go no more roaming far o'er the salt sea,
But I'll spend all my days with the little Mohee.

B[12]

"Mawee" is the title of this variant. Of the three
variants printed by Cox, one has the title, "Pretty
Maumee", another, "The Pretty Maumee," and still
another, "The Little Maumee." Perhaps "Mawee" is
a corruption of "Maumee."

As I was a-walking for pleasure one day
In a sweeter creation I happened to stray,
And as I sat 'musing myself in the grass,
It is who should come nigh me but an Indian lass.

She came and sat down by me, took hold of my hand,
Saying, "You look like a stranger, not one of this
　　land.
But if you will follow, you are welcome to come,
Though I live by myself, Sir, in a snug little home."

Together we rambled; together we roamed
Till at last we came near to that Indian home.
She opened the door, and she bid me come in,
And she treated me kindly to all that was in.

Saying, "Never go roaming across the salt sea,
And I teach you the language of little Mawee."
"Oh, no, my pretty fair maid, that never could be,
For I have a true love in my own country,

"And I promised to wed her for her loyalty,
And her heart beats as truly as yours, Mawee.
My ship is all ready and I must away,
For I have but once more for to cross the salt sea."

The last time I saw her was down at the strand,
And as I passed by her, she waved me her hand,
Saying,"When you get home to the girl that you love,
Just think of Mawee and the stranger from home."

It was soon that I land on my own native shore;
My friends and relations came 'round me once more,
But none that comes 'round me and none that I see
Can compare with my little Mawee.

21

JOHNNY SANDS[13]

For textual comparison see Pound, no. 48. (The central incident [fourth stanza] links this song with *The Old Woman from Slab City.*—J.W.A.)

Johnny Sands

A man whose name was Johnny Sands,
That married Betty Hague,
Although she brought him gold and land,
She proved a terrible plague,
She proved a terrible plague.

Says he, "Then I will drown myself;
The river runs below."
"I pray you do, you silly elf;
I wished it long ago,
I wished it long ago."

"For fear that I should courage lack
And try to save my life,
Pray tie my hands behind my back."
"I will," replied his wife,
"I will," replied his wife.

She tied them fast as you might think,
And when securely done,
"Now stand here upon the brink,
While I prepare to run,
While I prepare to run."

All down the hill his loving bride
Now ran with all her force
To push him in. He stepped aside,
And she fell in, of course,
And she fell in, of course.

Oh, splashing, dashing like a fish,
"Oh, save me, Johnny Sands!"
"I can't, my dear, though much I wish,
For you have tied my hands,
For you have tied my hands."

22

WILL RAY[14]

This is not a widely known ballad in Egypt; nor do I find it in any of the ballad collections that I have examined.

Will Ray

Oh, Papa, dear Papa, do tell me
Just what you think of Will Ray,
And if he should ask for your daughter,
Oh, Papa dear, what would you say?

Oh, Daughter dear, how you do shock me
To think you so handsome and gay
Would offer to stoop from your level
To marry that pauper, Will Ray.

But, Daughter, I've something to tell you;
Now listen and mind what I say.
You know Johnny Burns, the rich banker;
He's coming to see you today.

Yes, Daughter, young Johnny is coming
To claim you, my dear, as his wife,
And you shall have satins and jewels
And be the bright star of his life.

But, Papa, young Burns has not asked me,
And if he should what should I say?
My heart is not mine to be given;
'Tis already given away.

But, Papa, I've something to tell you;
'Tis something about Johnny Burns;
His wealth has all vanished and left him;
How the wheel of fortune does turn!

And, Papa, I've more for to tell you;
'Tis something about Willie Ray.
His uncle has died and has left him
A cool hundred thousand, they say.

But, Daughter, you must not expect him;
Now listen and mind what I say;
Listen to Johnny no longer,
But marry that wealthy Will Ray.

Then, Daughter, I want you to marry
Your handsome lover, Will Ray,
And shine in your satins and jewels
And be the bright star of his day.

But, Papa, young Burns is so lonely,
And his loss makes him feel very sad.
He has asked me to marry him, Papa,
And his losses also make me feel bad.

But, Papa, there's no use in talking;
It's hard for to tame a wild herd;
I have promised to marry him, Papa,
And I'll never go back on my word.

NOTES ON CHAPTER IV

1. Secured from Miss Edna Dunn, Metropolis, Illinois, who got it from her aunt, Mrs. Minnie Trovillian of Brownfield. Mrs. Trovillian learned it from her mother, Mrs. A. B. Bland, also of Brownfield, whose family brought it from Tennessee. The music was furnished by Miss Dunn.

2. This ballad I copied from the manuscript book belonging to the Watson and James families, who live near Carterville. It is one of the ballads that they love to sing and play.

3. Obtained by Mr. William H. Creed, Belleville, from the manuscript book belonging to Mrs. Clara Walpert of Belleville.

4. Miss Louise Atkinson, Salem, secured a manuscript of this song for me from her aunt, Mrs. Hattie Bitner of Waltonville.

5. Mr. Dave H. Adamson, Belleville, gave me this ballad, which he had obtained from Charles Pear, a student in his school.

6. Mr. William H. Creed copied this ballad for me from the manuscript book of Mrs. Clara Walpert of Belleville.

7. Mr. Dave H. Adamson, Belleville, copied this from the singing of his mother, Mrs. D. H. Adamson, Sr., also of Belleville.

8. Miss Dorothy Westwood, Belleville, gave me this ballad, which she learned from her father.

9. This ballad was copied from a manuscript belonging to Mrs. Hattie Bitner, Waltonville, which Miss Louise Atkinson, Salem, borrowed for me.

10. Miss Julia Mason, Belleville, copied this from Miss Belle Steurnagel, a librarian of Belleville, who remembered it from her mother's singing.

11. Miss Alice Story, Harrisburg, Illinois, gave me this ballad, which she had heard her mother and sisters sing.

12. Obtained by Mr. William H. Creed, Belleville, from the manuscript book of Mrs. Clara Walpert, of that city.

13. This also was secured by Mr. William H. Creed, Belleville, from Mrs. Clara Walpert's manuscript book. The music was copied from the singing of Mrs. Walpert.

14. Mr. William H. Creed copied this from the manuscript book belonging to Mrs. Clara Walpert. The music was taken down from the singing of Mrs. Walpert.

CHAPTER V

WESTERN SONGS

COMPARATIVELY few Western songs seem to be current in Egypt. One can hardly account for their scarcity on the ground that there was little or no communication between Egypt and the West. From the Civil War until fairly recent times young men from this section went West to seek their fortunes, and a good many of them returned. Others fled to the West as fugitives from justice; among them were certain individuals involved in the Bloody Vendetta of Williamson County. These fugitives grew weary of their journey and returned to serve their sentences, but none of them appears to have brought back songs, though they loved to tell of their travels.

One Western song enjoys a fairly general popularity; it is "The Dying Cowboy." Its popularity may be the result of its sentimentality, for the sentimental song has a widespread vogue among the lovers of ballads and folk-songs in southern Illinois.

23

THE DYING COWBOY

See Pound, no. 77, and Lomax, *Cowboy Songs*, pp. 74–76, for a comparison of texts.

A[1]

As I passed by Tom Sherman's barroom,
Tom Sherman's barroom so early one day,
'Twas there I espied a handsome young cowboy
All robed in white linen as if for the grave.

Chorus

So beat the drums lowly; play the fife slowly
Play the death march as they carry me along.
Take me to the graveyard and lay the sod o'er me;
I'm only a poor cowboy; I know I've done wrong.

'Twas once in my saddle I used to go dashing;
'Twas once in my saddle I used to go gay.
I first took to drinking, and then took to gambling,
Got shot in the breast, and now I must die.

Oh, break the news to my gray-headed mother;
Oh, take the sad news to my sister so fair;
But never one word of misfortune to mention
As they gather around you my story to hear.

But then there's another more dear than a sister
Who vainly will weep when she hears I am gone,
But then there's another to win her affection,
For I am only a poor cowboy; I know I've done
    wrong.

He asked them to bring him a cup of cold water
To bathe his temples, the poor fellow said.
But when they returned it the spirit had left him,
Had gone to the Giver; the cowboy was dead.

B²

As I went down to Tom Canian's bar room
So early one day,
I met a charming young cowboy
All dressed in white linen and ready to die.

Beat your drums lowly.
And play your fifes slowly,
And play the Dead March
While you carry him away.

"Take me to the prairie
And lay the sod o'er me,
For I'm a poor cowboy
And know I've did wrong.

"Write a letter to the gray-headed mother,
One to my sister, so kindly, so true.
There is one that's dearer than sister or mother.
How sad she would be if she knew I was here.

How sad she would be if she knew I was here.
"Once in my saddle I used to go dashing;
Once in my saddle I used to ride gay;
I first got to drinking and then to card playing
Got shot in the breast and am dying today.

"Bring me some water, a cup of cold water,
A cup of cold water," the poor cowboy said.
When I got to him, the spirit had left him,
And gone to his Maker—the cowboy was dead.

C³

As I rode so early, so early, o'er there,
. . . .
I saw a cowboy all dressed in white linen,
With coal black eyes and wavy brown hair.

. . . .
. . . .
I first went to Texas and hired as a gunman,
Got shot in the bosom, and death is my doom.

Go break the news to my gray-haired mother
And . . . . . . my sister so dear,
But there is another who's dearer than Mother,
Who would weep if she knew I was dying out here.

So . . . . . play the fife slowly,

. . . .

. . . . and place the sod o'er me,

For I'm a dead cowboy, and I know I've done
wrong.

24

WHOOPEE, TO YI YO[4]

Compare with Pound, no. 80, and Lomax, *Cowboy Songs*, pp. 87–88.

As I was out walking one morning for pleasure
I met a young cowboy just strolling along;
His hat was throwed back and his spurs were
a-jingling
And he approached me a-singing this song:

Refrain:

Whoopee, ti yi, yo, git along, little dogies,
It's your misfortune and none of my own.
Whoopee, ti, yi, yo, git along, little dogies,
For you know Wyoming will be your new home.

Early in the spring we round up the dogies,
Mark them and brand them and bob off their tails,
Round up our horses, load up the chuck wagon,
Then throw the dogies up on the trail.

It's whooping and yelling and driving the dogies;
O how I wish that they would go on,
It's whooping and punching, go on, little dogies,
For you know Wyoming will be your new home.

When the night comes on we herd them on the led
ground,
These little dogies that roll so slow;
Roll up the herd and cut out the strays
And roll the little dogies that never rolled before.

If ever I marry t'will be to a widow
With six little orphans and none of my own;
If ever I marry 'twill be to a widow
With a great big ranch and a ten-story home.

25

JOE BOWERS[5]

For comparison see Pound, no. 88 and Lomax, *Cowboy Songs*, pp. 15–17.

My name is Joe Bowers;
I've got a brother Ike;
I came from Old Missouri,
All the way from Pike;
I'll tell you why I left thar,
And why I came to roam,
And leave my poor old mammy
So far away from home:

I used to court a gal thar;
Her name was Sally Black;
I axed her if she'd marry me;
She said it was a whack;
Says she to me, "Joe Bowers,
Before we hitch for life,
You ought to get a little home
To keep your little wife."

Oh, Sally! Dearest Sally!
Oh, Sally, for your sake
I'll go to California
And try to raise a stake;
Says she to me, "Joe Bowers,
You are the man to win;
Here's a kiss to bind the bargain,"
And she hove a dozen in.

When I got in that country,
I hadn't nary red;
I had such wolfish feelings,
I wished myself 'most dead;
But the thought of my dear Sally
Soon made them feelings git,
And whisper hopes to Bowers;
I wish I had 'em yit.

At length I went to mining,
Put in my biggest licks,
Went down upon the boulders
Just like a thousand bricks;
I worked both late and early,
In rain, in sun, in snow,
I was working for my Sally
'Twas all the same to Joe.

At length I got a letter
From my dear brother Ike;
It came from Old Missouri,
All the way from Pike.
It brought to me the darndest news
That ever you did hear;
My heart is almost bustin',
So pray excuse this tear.

It said that Sal was false to me;
Her love for me had fled;
She'd got married to a butcher;
The butcher's hair was red;
And more than that the letter said—
It's enough to make me swear—
That Sally had a baby;
The baby had red hair.

Now, I've told you all
About this said affair,
'Bout Sally marrying a butcher,
That butcher with red hair.
But whether 'twas a boy or gal child
The letter never said;
It only said the baby's hair
Was inclined to be red.

26

THE FARM IN THE WEST[6]

I've a farm out in the West,
Where the farms they are the best.
I've a cross-eyed mule with freckles and red
    hair.
I have one old Texas steer,
With a wart on his left ear.
But he's dead now and climbed the Golden
    Stair.

But my poor old Shanghai rooster,
Who in battle nobly fell;
With O'Brien's bulldog he fought long and
    brave.
And the only thing that keeps me
From going out and getting drunk
Is a feather from my Shanghai rooster's grave.

His comb was like a toothbrush,
And his spur was like an adz.
And his tombstone was a sugar hogshead
    stave.
And the only thing that keeps me
From going out and getting drunk
Is a feather from my Shanghai rooster's grave.

No more he'll come home late
At the hour of half-past-eight,
Singing cock-a-doodle-doo and good-bye, Jake.
No more he'll dodge the brickbats
Thrown at some old tom-cat,
Or flirt with chicken pullets at the gate.

.   .   .   .
.   .   .   .
.   .   .   .

His wife is in the boneyard,
Sitting on a lump of coal;
She's weeping o'er my Shanghai rooster's
   grave.

NOTES ON CHAPTER V

1. Communicated by Mr. William H. Creed, Belleville, who got it from the manuscript book of Mrs. Clara Walpert of Belleville.

2. Copied from the singing of Mr. Fred Kirby, of Flora, who had learned it from his mother.

3. Secured from Miss Hallie Eubanks, Belleville.

4. Obtained from Miss Dorothy Westwood, Belleville, who learned it from her father, the late Edward Westwood.

5. Communicated by Miss Emilie Huck, New Baden, who secured it from Miss Catherine Kettler. Miss Kettler learned it from an old broadside which had been in the family for several generations.

6. Secured from Miss Helen Piper, Oakdale, who copied it from the singing of her father.

CHAPTER VI

NURSERY AND GAME SONGS

IN SOUTHERN Illinois thirty or forty years ago play parties were a favorite means of entertainment in certain rural sections. After they had lost their popularity, people still continued to sing the songs to which the games had been played—songs that are rapidly losing their significance to the younger generations. Such songs as "Skip To My Lou" and "Weevily Wheat" continue to enjoy a wide popularity, in many cases among people who know little or nothing of the games for which they were sung.

Game-songs of childhood are still sung to the games for which they were intended. In part, that fact may result from the efforts of teachers to keep children entertained on the school grounds; such is likely to be the case especially in town and cities. In rural schools the game-song is still the heritage of the young.

Of the nursery songs, "Billy Boy" has a currency that has scarcely been circumscribed by time. Most people, both young and old, know its tune, and there are very few who cannot remember one or more of its stanzas. "In the Old Colony Times" or "The Three Rogues" is less familiar than "Billy Boy," the delight of my childhood.

27

IN THE GOOD OLD COLONY DAYS[1]

This song seems not to have a wide circulation in Egypt. In other sections it goes under different titles; Pound (*Ballads*, no. 116) calls it "In Good Old Colony Times"; Cox (*Folk-Songs of the South*, no. 166) calls it

"The Three Rogues" and observes that there are two variants in West Virginia.

For a comparison of Texts see Pound and Cox.

In the good old colony days
When I lived under the king,
Three roguish little chaps fell into mishaps
Because they could not sing.
Oh, the first he was a weaver,

And the second he was a miller,
And the third he was a little tailor boy—
Three roguish chaps together.

Oh, the weaver he stole yarn,
And the miller he stole corn,
And the little tailor boy he stole broadcloth
To keep these three rogues warm.

Oh, the miller got drown in his dam,
And the weaver got hung in his yarn,
And the devil clapped his claw on the little
    tailor boy,
With the broadcloth under his arm.

28

BILLY BOY

"Billy Boy" has a wide circulation in Southern Illinois.

See Pound, no. 113, Cox, no. 168, and Lomax, *American Ballads and Folk-Songs*, pp. 320–322.

A²

"Where have you been, Billy Boy, Billy Boy?
Where have you been charming Billy?"
"I have been to seek a wife; she's the joy of my life;
She's a young thing and cannot leave her mother."

"Did she bid you in, Billy Boy, Billy Boy?
Did she bid you in charming Billy?"
"Yes, she bid me in with a dimple in her chin;
She's a young thing and cannot leave her mother."

"Did she set for you a chair, Billy Boy, Billy Boy?
Did she set for you a chair, charming Billy?"
"Yes, she set for me a chair with a look up in the air;
She's a young thing and cannot leave her mother."

"Can she bake a cherry pie, Billy Boy, Billy Boy?
Can she bake a cherry pie, charming Billy?"
"She can bake a cherry pie quick as cat can wink her
    eye;
She's a young thing and cannot leave her mother."

"How old is she, Billy Boy, Billy Boy?
How old is she, charming Billy?"
"She's twice six, twice seven, twice forty and eleven;
She's a young thing and cannot leave her mother."

B³

"Oh, where have you been Billy Boy, Billy Boy?
Oh where have you been, charming William?"
"I have been to see my wife; she's the dear thing of
    my life;
Oh, she's a young thing and cannot leave her
    mother."

"Did she set for you a chair, Billy Boy, Billy Boy?
Did she set for you a chair, charming William?"
"Yes, she set for me a chair with a look up in the air;
Oh, she's a young thing and cannot leave her
    mother."

"Can she bake a cherry pie, Billy Boy, Billy Boy?
Can she bake a cherry pie, charming William?"
She can bake a cherry pie quick as a cat can wink its
    eye;
Oh, she's a young thing and cannot leave her
    mother."

"How old is she, Billy Boy, Billy Boy?
How old is she, charming William?"
"Twice six, twice seven, twice twenty, twice eleven;
Oh, she's a young thing and cannot leave her
    mother."

29

PAPER OF PINS

Compare with Pound, no. 111 and Lomax, *American
Ballads and Folk-Songs*, pp. 323-324. (Ultimately British?—J.W.A.)

The first variant of the ballad is known by the title
"If You Will Marry Me"; the second, by "Paper of
pins."

Paper of Pins

A⁴

I will give you a paper of pins
If that's the way true love begins,
If you will marry me, me, me,
If you will marry me.

Chorus:

I'll not accept of your paper of pins;
That's not the way true love begins;
And I'll not marry you, you, you,
And I'll not marry you.

I'll give you a little black dog
To follow you when you go abroad,
If you will marry me, me, me,
If you will marry me.

I will give you a dress in red
All bound around with golden thread,
If you will marry me, me, me,
If you will marry me.

I will give you a dress in green
To make you look like a queen,
If you will marry me, me, me,
If you will marry me.

I will give you the key of my heart
That you and I may never part,
If you will marry me, me, me,
If you will marry me.

I will give you the key of my chest
That you can have money at your request,
If you will marry me, me, me,
If you will marry me.

I'll give you the key to my heart
That you and I will never part,
If you will marry me, me, me,
If you will marry me.

B[5]

I'll give you a paper of pins
If you will marry me, me, me.
I'll not accept your paper of pins,
And I'll not marry you, you, you,
And I'll not marry you.

I'll give to you a little lap dog,
To go with you when you go abroad,
If you will marry me, me, me,
If you will marry me.

I'll not accept your little lap dog,
To go with me when I go abroad,
And I'll not marry you, you, you,
And I'll not marry you.

I'll give to you a coach and four
With every horse as white as snow,
If you will marry me, me, me,
If you will marry me.

I'll not accept your coach and four
With every horse as white as snow,
And I'll not marry you, you, you
And I'll not marry you.

I'll give to you a coach and six
With every horse as black as pitch,
If you will marry me, me, me,
If you will marry me.

I'll not accept your coach and six
With every horse as black as pitch,
And I'll not marry you, you, you,
And I'll not marry you.

I'll give to you the key to my heart
That we may lock and never part,
If you will marry me, me, me,
If you will marry me.

I'll not accept the key to your heart
That we may lock and never part,
And I'll not marry you, you, you,
And I'll not marry you.

I'll give to you a chest of gold,
And all the money you can control,
If you will marry me, me, me,
If you will marry me.

I'll not accept your chest of gold,
And all the money I can control,
And I'll not marry you, you, you,
And I'll not marry you.

Ha! Ha! Ha! Ha! Money is all;
Woman's love is nothing at all,
And I'll not marry you, you, you,
And I'll not marry you.

30

POOR ROBIN

See Pound, no. 114 and Fuson, *Ballads of the Kentucky Highlands*, p. 186.

"Poor Robin" is the title of the first variant; "Old Johnny" that of the second.

Old Johnny

A⁶

Poor Robin is dead and laid in his grave,
Laid in his grave, laid in his grave,
Poor Robin is dead and laid in his grave,
O, O, O.

There grew an old apple tree over his head,
Over his head, over his head,
There grew an old apple tree over his head,
O, O, O.

The apples got ripe and ready to drop,
Ready to drop, ready to drop,
The apples got ripe and ready to drop,
O, O, O.

There came an old woman a-picking them up,
A-picking them up, a-picking them up,
There came an old woman a-picking them up,
O, O, O.

Old Robin got up and gave her a thump,
And gave her a thump, and gave her a thump,
Old Robin got up and gave her a thump,
O, O, O.

It made the old woman go hippety hop,
Go hippety hop, go hippety hop,
It made the old woman go hippety hop,
O, O, O.

B⁷

OLD JOHNNY

Old Johnny was dead and lay in his grave,
Lay in his grave, lay in his grave,
Old Johnny was dead and lay in his grave,
A long time ago.

There grew an old apple tree over his head,
Over his head, over his head,
There grew an old apple tree over his head,
A long time ago.

When the apples were ripe and beginning to fall,
Beginning to fall, beginning to fall,
When the apples were ripe and beginning to fall,
A long time ago;

There came an old woman and picked them up,
Picked them up, picked them up,
There came an old woman and picked them up,
A long time ago.

Old Johnny jumped up and gave her a kick,
Gave her a kick, gave her a kick,
Old Johnny jumped up and gave her a kick,
A long time ago.

It made the old woman go hippity hop,
Hippity hop, hippity hop,
It made the old woman go hippity hop,
A long time ago.

31

HAPPY IS THE MILLER[8]

This is a game that the children used to play in Egypt
not many years ago.

Happy is the miller that lives by the mill,
Ever time the mill turns, turns to his will.
Hand on the hopper, the other on the slab;
Every time the mill turns, grab, boys, grab!

32

THE PIG IN THE PARLOR[9]

My parents used to play a game to this song, but I
know it simply as a song my mother often sang.
Compare the text with Pound, no. 119.

> My father and mother were Irish,
> My father and mother were Irish,
> My father and mother were Irish,
>> And I am Irish, too,
>> And I am Irish, too,
> My father and mother were Irish,
> My father and mother were Irish,
> My father and mother were Irish,
>> And I am Irish, too.

Chorus

> Your right hand to your partner,
> Your left hand to your neighbor,
> Your right hand to your partner,
>> And all promenade,
>> And all promenade,
> Your right hand to your partner,
> Your left hand to your neighbor,
> Your right hand to your partner,
>> And all promenade.

> They fed the pig in the parlor,
> They fed the pig in the parlor,
> They fed the pig in the parlor,
>> And that was Irish, too,
>> And that was Irish, too,
> They fed the pig in the parlor,
> They fed the pig in the parlor,
> They fed the pig in the parlor,
>> And that was Irish, too.

We have a new pig in the parlor,
We have a new pig in the parlor,
We have a new pig in the parlor,
   And it is Irish, too,
   And it is Irish, too,
We have a new pig in the parlor,
We have a new pig in the parlor,
We have a new pig in the parlor,
   And it is Irish, too.

33

KING WILLIAM WAS KING JAMES'S SON

Thirty-five or forty years ago the young folk in certain parts of Egypt used to play a game to this song. The game was disapproved of by the older people because it was a kissing game.

A^{10}

King William was King James's son;
When the royal race he won,
He wore a star upon his breast,
To conquer East and to conquer West.

Go choose your East, go choose your West,
Choose the one that you love best;
If they're not here to take their part,
Choose another with all your heart.

Down on this carpet you must kneel,
Sure as the grass grows in the field;
So choose your bride and kiss her sweet;
Now you may rise upon your feet.

B[11]

King William was King James's son;
Upon a royal race he run.
He wore a star upon his breast,
Called the star of the Indian West.

Come choose your East, come choose your West,
Come choose the one which you love best;
If she's not there, come take your part,
And choose another with all your heart.

34

WEEVILY WHEAT

Formerly popular as a game-song, this is now sung simply as a folk-song.

See for a comparison of texts Lomax, *American Ballads and Folk Songs*, pp. 290–293 and Sandburg, *The American Songbag*, p. 161.

A[12]

Charlie he's a handsome man,
Charlie he's a dandy;
He knows how to feed the girls,
On pretty striped candy.

Chorus:

I won't have none of your weevily wheat,
I won't have none of your barley,
But the best of flour and a half an hour,
And I'll bake a cake for Charlie.

Oh, do come along, my pretty little miss,
Oh, do come along, my honey;
Oh, do come along, my pretty little miss
And promenade with Charlie.

Come trip with me, my pretty little miss,
Come trip with me, my honey;
Come trip with me, my pretty little miss;
I'll be sixteen next Sunday.

How old are you, my pretty little miss,
How old are you, my honey?
She answered me with a "Tee, hee, hee"
"I'll be sixteen next Sunday."

B[13]

Charlie he's a nice young man,
Charlie he's a dandy;
Charlie loves to swing the girls,
For swinging comes so handy.

Chorus:

I won't have none of your weevily wheat;
I won't have none of your barley.
Give me some flour in half an hour
To bake a cake for Charlie.

Come trip with me, my pretty little miss,
Come trip with me, my honey;
Come trip with me, my pretty little miss;
I'll be sixteen next Sunday.

35
SKIP TO MY LOU[14]

"Skip to my Lou" is still widely popular in Southern Illinois. I have frequently heard men sing it as they worked in the fields. From the singing of one farm hand this stanza was firmly fixed in my mind:

"If you can't get a red bird, a jay bird'll do,
If you can't get a red bird, a jay bird'll do,
If you can't get a red bird, a jay bird'll do;
Skip to my Lou, my darling."

See Lomax, *American Ballads and Folk Songs*, pp. 294–295.

My wife skipped, and I'll skip, too,
My wife skipped, and I'll skip, too,
My wife skipped, and I'll skip, too,
Skip to my Lou, my darling.

Rabbit on the hillside, kicking like a mule,
Rabbit on the hillside, kicking like a mule,
Rabbit on the hillside, kicking like a mule,
Skip to my Lou, my darling.

Hole in the haystack, chicken fell through,
Hole in the haystack, chicken fell through,
Hole in the haystack, chicken fell through,
Skip to my Lou, my darling.

Take her, keep her, I don't want her,
Take her, keep her, I don't want her,
Take her, keep her, I don't want her,
Skip to My Lou, my darling.

If I can't get a red bird, a blue bird will do,
If I can't get a red bird, a blue bird will do,
If I can't get a red bird, a blue bird will do,
Skip to my Lou, my darling.

I'll get me another, that's what I'll do,
I'll get me another, that's what I'll do,
I'll get me another, that's what I'll do,
Skip to my Lou, my darling.

Wheel broke down, the axle is dragging,
Wheel broke down, the axle is dragging,
Wheel broke down, the axle is dragging,
Skip to my Lou, my darling.

36

HOG AND HOMINY[15]

"Hog and Hominy" was a game-song, fairly well
known in southern Pope County thirty or forty years
ago. With the passing of the game, the song has lost its
popularity.

Here stands a loving couple;
Join heart and hand;
One wants a wife,
And the other wants a man.

They will get married,
If they can agree;
So it's march down the river
To hog and hominy.

And now they are married,
And since it is so,
Off to the war
My true-love has to go.

And it's weeping and wailing
That shall meet my ear;
If I never see my true-love,
Surely I shall die.

Oh, yonder he comes,
And it's "Howdy, howdy do.
How have you been
Since I parted from you?"

The war is all over,
And free from all harm,
Can't you give us joy
By the waving of your arms?

37

MARCHING ROUND THE LEVEE[16]

The game to which the song is sung was still popular among the young folk twenty years or so ago, especially in rural communities.

We're marching round the levee,
We're marching round the levee,
We're marching round the levee,
Since we have gained the day.

Go in and out the window,
Go in and out the window,
Go in and out the window,
Since we have gained the day.

Go forth and choose your lover,
Go forth and choose your lover,
Go forth and choose your lover,
Since we have gained the day.

I kneel because I love you,
I kneel because I love you,
I kneel because I love you,
Since we have gained the day.

One kiss and then I leave you,
One kiss and then I leave you,
One kiss and then I leave you,
Since we have gained the day.

38

A DANCE CALL

Almost as interesting as the game-songs are the calls for square dances. Forty or fifty years ago most rural neighborhoods had a number of individuals who were able to "call." I can remember, as a child, listening with fascination to the performance of one of these individuals down in Pope County, at the Jacobs Neighborhood along Alcorn Creek.

An acquaintance of my father's sent me two calls that he used forty-five or fifty years ago. With them he included a note to my father, in which he said: "Charley excuse this righting. I am doing this by lamp light. I am 66 years old. Never weair no glasses and I can see as well as I ever could. Back 45 and fifty years ago when I usto promp for a squair dance, this is what I said to them."

A¹⁷

Get your pardners on the floor.
Is everybody ready? Let's go.
Abedance to your pardner and to the lady on the left.
Swing your pardner.
Promnade the girl behind you till you get around;
Then swing her; then swing on your left;
Then give your pardner your right hand and go right
    and left,
And when you meet your pardner, swing her once and
    a half.
Swing all the girls alike, for the boys are all jels,
And when you meet your pardner, swing her.
Then the three gents swing his pardner
And promnade the girl behind him till you get around.
Swing her; then promnade the girl behind him.
Then the four gents to the right go through just the
    same way
As the other three gents did.
When he gets round, swing corners,
All first cupple to the cupple on the right.
Right hand across left hand.
Back serckel.
Four hands one half round.
Balance up to the next cupple.
Serckel four hands one half round.
When all four gents gets around, then swing your pard-
    ner.
Thank the ladys and kiss the fidlers.

39

LADY ROUND THE LADY[18]

All to your places.
All pich in.
Honor your pardner, the lady on the left.
Hands up and scearkle to the left.
Grand trail back.
Swing your pardner, the lady on the left.
Right hand to your pardner.
Grand right and left.
Wach your pardner; wach her clost.
When you meet your pardner, swing her once and a
    half.
Swing all the girls once and a half.
First lady go round the second cuple. The gents don't
    go.
The lady round the lady and gent solo.
Balance two to two.
Fore hands half round.
The ladys do-see-doe,
And the gents—you know—
"You swing my pardner, and I'll swing yours."
Balance to the next cuple.
Four hands swing half round.
Ladys do-see-doe.
The gents—you know.
Balance to the next cuple, seckent cuple to the right.
Lady round the gent, and the gent don't go.
All four cuples go round.
Then swing your pardner.
Promnade the girl behind you.
Treat all the girls alike.
Then meet your pardner.
Swing.
Promnade her to the lemonade stand.

NOTES ON CHAPTER VI

1. Sung by Mrs. Charles Neely, Sr., Carbondale, who learned it from her cousin, the late Mrs. Nina Crowe, New Liberty.

2. Secured from Mr. Dave H. Adamson, Belleville.

3. Obtained from Mrs. Charles Neely, Sr., Carbondale, who learned it from her cousin, the late Mrs. Nina Crowe, New Liberty.

4. Both the words and the music were secured from Mrs. Clara Walpert, Belleville.

5. Miss Rosalie Comment, Belleville, gave me the words to this song.

6. Obtained from Mrs. Harold G. Kaiser, Belleville.

7. Miss Anna Grommet, Belleville, gave me the words of this song, to which she played a game in her childhood.

8. Sung by Mrs. Charles Neely, Sr., Carbondale.

9. Secured from Mrs. Charles Neely, Sr., of Carbondale.

10. Obtained from Mrs. Charles Neely, Sr., of Carbondale, and Mrs. Elmer Garrett of Brookport.

11. Secured from Miss Anna Gromet of Belleville.

12. Obtained from Mr. and Mrs. Elmer Garrett of Brookport.

13. Sung by Mrs. Charles Neely, Sr., of Carbondale.

14. The words were obtained from Miss Inez Watson, Carterville. This is one of the songs in the Watson-James manuscript book.

15. Mr. and Mrs. Elmer Garrett of Brookport and Mrs. Charles Neely, Sr., of Carbondale, by their joint efforts gave me this song.

16. Secured from Mrs. Charles Neely, Sr., Carbondale.

17. Communicated by Mr. James T. Johnson, Brookport.

18. Communicated by Mr. James T. Johnson, Brookport.

CHAPTER VII

MISCELLANY

IN THIS chapter I have included such recognized folk-songs as "Abdul da Bool Bool de Meer" ("Ye Ballade of Ivan Petrofsky Skevar") and "William Stafford" with popular songs that have passed into oral tradition such as "Break the News to Mother," "A Hot Time in the Old Town," "Old Grimes Is Dead," and "Grandfather's Clock." I have included also minstrel pieces such as "Billy's Dream" and "Bill Bailey." The songs and minstrel pieces are sung without any knowledge of the name of the author; and, depending mainly upon oral tradition for transmission, they show the variations which take place in ballads and folk-songs. In a sense, one may argue that they are true folk-pieces, for the folk have incorporated them in their lore.

40

ABDUL DA BOOL BOOL DE MEER[1]

Compare with Lomax, *American Ballads and Folk Songs*, pp. 341–343, and Sandburg, *The American Song-bag*, pp. 344–346.

The sons of a seer are both brave and bold
  And wholly unknowing of fear.
But the greatest of all was a man who was called
  Abdul da Bool Bool de Meer.

That son of the desert in battle engaged
  Could split twenty men on a spear.
A dangerous creature when calm or enraged
  Was Abdul da Bool Bool de Meer.

There are brave men in plenty, well known as to fame,
   In the army that's run by the czar.
But the bravest of all was a man who by name
   Was Ivan Skevinsky Skevar.

The ladies all loved him, his rivals were few,
   He'd drink them all under the bar.
As empty a tank, none with him could rank
   With this Ivan Skevinsky Skevar.

"Young man," said de Meer, "is existence so slow
   That you hanker to end your career?
For, fool, you must know you've trod on the toe
   Of great Abdul da Bool Bool de Meer."

"I'll tread on your toes whenever I choose,"
   Said Ivan who'd never known fear,
And with quickly aimed gun put a stop to the fun
   Of Abdul da Bool Bool de Meer.

Then Gotchski, Skabelski, Menchiski, too,
   Saw how pierced was Ivan's young heart,
Were only in time to bid deathly adieu
   To gay Ivan Skevinsky Skevar.

Now, stranger, remember to pray for the soul
   Of Abdul da Bool Bool de Meer.
For there's many a maiden who wails soft and low
   For Young Ivan Skevinsky Skevar.

41

WILLIAM STAFFORD[2]

See Cox, *Folk-Songs of the South*, no. 52, and Lomax,
Cowboy Songs, pp. 226–228. Cox printed the song under
the title, "An Arkansaw Traveller" and "Bill Stafford";
Lomax, under the title, "The State of Arkansaw."

My name is William Stafford,
  Was raised in Boston Town;
For nine years as a rover
  I roved the wide world 'round;
Through all its ups and downs
  Some bitter days I saw,
But never knew what misery was
  Till I struck Arkansaw.

I started on my journey,
  'Twas the merry month of June;
I landed in New Jersey
  One sultry afternoon.
Along came a walking skeleton
  With long and lantern jaw.
He asked me to his hotel
  In the state of Arkansaw.

I followed up a great long rope
  Into his boarding place,
Where hunger and starvation
  Were printed on his face;
His bread it was corn dodger;
  His beef I could not chaw;
He taxed me fifty cents for that
  In the state of Arkansaw.

I rose the next morning early
  To catch the early train.
He said, "Young man, you'd better stay;
  I have some land to drain.
I'll give you fifty cents a day,
  Your washing, board, and all;
You'll find yourself a different lad
  When you leave Arkansaw."

Six months I worked for this galoot;
  Charles Tyler was his name;
He was six feet seven in his boots
  And thin as any crane.
His hair hung down like rat tails
  Around his lantern jaw;
He was the photograph of all the gents
  That's raised in Arkansaw.

He fed me on corn dodgers
  As hard as any rock;
My teeth began to loosen;
  My knees began to knock.
I got so thin on sassafras,
  Could hide behind a straw,
So I sho' was a different lad
  When I left Arkansaw.

42

BREAK THE NEWS TO MOTHER[3]

See Sigmund G. Spaeth, *Read 'Em and Weep* (New York, 1926), pp. 194–195, for a comparison of texts and for an account of the composition of the song. Though it deals with an imaginary incident of the Civil War, its popularity dates from the Spanish-American War.

When the shot and shells were screaming upon a battle
    field,
The boys in blue were fighting their noble flag to shield.
Came a cry from our brave captain, "Look, boys, our
    flag is down!
Who'll volunteer and save it from disgrace?"
"I will," a young voice shouted. "I'll bring it back
    or die."
And he sprang into the thickest of the spray.
Saved the flag, but gave his own young life all for his
    country's sake.
They brought him back and softly heard him say:

Chorus:

"Just break the news to Mother,
For she knows how dear I love her;
Just tell her not to wait for me,
For I'm not coming home.
Just say there is no other
Can take the place of Mother;
Just kiss her dear sweet lips for me
And break the news to her."

From afar a noted general had witnessed that brave
deed.
"Who saved the flag? Speak up, lad; was noble, brave,
indeed."
"Here he lies, sir," said the captain. "He's sinking very
fast."
And he slowly turned away to hide a tear.
"'Tis my son, my own brave hero; I thought you was
safe at home."
"Forgive me, Father, for I run away."

43

A HOT TIME IN THE OLD TOWN[4]

Made popular during the Spanish-American War,
this song still has a fairly wide circulation in Southern
Illinois. Many people are able to sing snatches of it,
and perhaps many more know the tune.

For comparison of texts see Dailey Paskman and
Sigmund G. Spaeth, *Gentlemen, Be Seated!* (New York,
1928), p. 98, and Spaeth, *Read 'Em and Weep*, pp. 222–
223.

Come along, get you ready; wear your bran' bran'
    new gown,
For der's gwine to be a meeting in that good, good
    old town,
Where you knowd ev'rybody and dey all knowd you;
And you've got a rabbit's foot to keep away the
    hoodoo.
When you hear that the preacher does begin,
Bend low down for to drive away your sin,
And when you gets religion, you want to shout and
    sing,
"There'll be a hot time in the old town tonight, my
    baby."

Chorus

When you hear dem bells go ding, ling, ling,
All join 'round and sweetly you must sing,
And when the verse am through an' the chorus all
    join in,
There'll be a hot time in the old town tonight.

There'll be girls for everybody in that good, good
    old town,
For there's Miss Consula Davis, an' there's Miss
    Gondolia Brown,
And there's Miss Jihanna Beasley, she am all dressed
    in red;
I just hugged her and I kissed her and to me then
    she said:
"Please, oh, please, oh, do not let me fall;
You're all mine and I love you best of all.
And you must be my man, or I'll have no man at all;
There'll be a hot time in the old town tonight, my
    baby."

44

BILLY'S DREAM[5]

According to Paskman and Spaeth, *Gentlemen, Be Seated!*, pp. 74-86, this song was the star number of Billy Arnold's repertoire.

I had a fight with Satan last night,
As I lay me half awake.
Ole Satan came to my bedside,
And he began to shake.
Oh, he shook me long, and he shook me
    strong,
And he shook me clear out of bed;
He grabbed me by the collar, and he looked
    me in the face,
And what do you think he said?

Chorus

"There's gold in the mountain,
And there's silver in the mine,
And it all belongs to you, Uncle Billy,
If you only will be mine."

. . . .
. . . .
. . . .
. . . .
. . . .
. . . .

And I grabbed him by the collar, and I looked
    him in the face,
And what do you think I said?

Chorus

"Get you gone, oh Satan;
You came to me to kill.
You might fool white folks with your trash,
But you can't fool poor black Bill."

Oh, I was feelin' quite chilly and thought I
    might catch cold;
So I crept into my bed,
And through the night I saw the good Lord
    his head.
Ole Satan had vanished through the floor,
. . . .
. . . .

And the Lord to me he said:

Chorus

"Well done, my faithful servant;
You can sit on my right hand,
Play on the golden harp all day,
Although you are a poor colored man."

45

BILL BAILEY[6]

On one summer's day the sun was shining fine;
The lady love of old Bill Bailey was hanging clothes
    on de line
In her back yard and weeping hard;
She married a B. & O. brakeman dat took and
    throw'd her down,
Bellering like a prune-fed calf, wid a big gang hang-
    ing 'round
And to dat crowd she yelled out loud:

Chorus

"Won't you come home, Bill Bailey, won't you
    come home!"
She moans de whole day long;
"I'll do de cooking, darling, I'll pay de rent;
I know I've done you wrong.
'Member dat rainy eve dat I drove you out
Wid nothing but a fine-tooth comb?
I knows I'se to blame; well, ain't dat a shame—
Bill Bailey, won't you please come home?"

Bill drove by dat door in an automobile,
A great big diamond, coach, and footman; hear dat
    big woman squeal;
"He's all alone," I heard her groan;
She hollered through dat door: "Bill Bailey is pop
    sure!
Stop a minute, won't you listen to me, won't I see
    you no more?"
Bill winked his eye as he heard her say:

Chorus

46

OLD GRIMES IS DEAD[7]

Compare with Cox, no. 170, and with Spaeth, *Weep
Some More, My Lady* (New York, 1927), pp. 150–151.

    Old Grimes is dead, that good old man;
    We nare shall see him more.
    He used to wear a long black coat
    All buttoned up before.

    His heart was open as the day;
    His feelings all were true.
    His hair it was inclined to gray;
    He wore it in a queue.

When'er he heard the voice of pain,
His heart with pity burned.
The large round head upon his cane
From ivory was turned.

Kind words he ever had for all;
He knew no base design.
His eyes were dark and rather small;
His nose was aquiline.

He lived at peace with all mankind;
In friendship he was true.
His coat had pocket holes behind;
His pantaloons were blue.

Unharmed with sin which earth pollutes,
He passed securely o'er
And never wore a pair of boots
For thirty years or more.

But good old Grimes is now at rest,
Nor fears misfortune's frown.
He wore a double breasted vest
With stripes run up and down.

He modest merit sought to find
And pay it its deserts.
He had no malice in his mind,
No ruffles on his shirt.

His neighbors he did not abuse,
Was sociable and gay.
He wore long buckles on his shoes
And changed them every day.

His knowledge hid from public gaze
He did not bring to view,
Nor make a noise town-meeting days
As many people do.

His worldly goods he never threw
Or left to fortune, chances;
He lived as all his brothers did
In easy circumstances.

Thus undisturbed by anxious cares
His peaceful moments ran,
And everybody said he was
A fine old gentleman.

47

GRANDFATHER'S CLOCK

Written by Henry C. Work, "Grandfather's Clock"
has become a folk-song by adoption, and it has begun
to show the effects of oral transmission.

A^8

My grandfather's clock was too tall for the
    shelf,
  So it stood ninety years on the floor;
It was taller by half than the old man himself,
  Though it weighed not a pennyweight more.
It was bought on the morn of the day he was born,
  And was always his treasure and pride,
But it stopped short, never to go again,
  When the old man died.

Chorus

Ninety years without slumbering—tick, tuck,
    tick, tuck,
  His life seconds numbering—tick, tick, tick,
    tick;
It stopped short, never to go again,
  When the old man died.

In watching its pendulum swing to and fro,
  Many hours had he spent when a boy,
And in childhood and manhood the clock seemed
      to keep
  And to share both his grief and his joy;
For it struck twenty-four when he entered the
      door,
  With a blooming and beautiful bride,
But it stopped short, never to go again,
  When the old man died.

My grandfather said that those he could hire
  Not a servant so faithful he found,
For it wasted no time and had but one desire
  At the close of each day to be wound.
It kept in its place, not a frown on its face,
  And its hands never hung by its side.
But it stopped short, never to run again,
  When the old man died.

B⁹

My grandfather's clock was too tall for the shelf,
  So it stood ninety years on the floor.
It was taller by far than the old man himself,
  Yet it weighed not a penny-weight more.

It was bought upon the morn of the day that he
      was born.
  All his life 'twas his joy and his pride.
But it stopped short, never to go again,
  When the old man died.

Ninety years without slumbering, tick-tock, tick-
      tock,
  Seconds, minutes numbering, tick-tock, tick-
      tock,
And it stopped short, never to go again,
  When the old man died.

NOTES ON CHAPTER VII

1. Obtained from Miss Julia Mason, Belleville.

2. Secured from Mr. Dave H. Adamson, Jr., Belleville, who learned it from his mother, Mrs. D. H. Adamson, Sr., of Belleville.

3. Copied from a manuscript belonging to Mrs. Hattie Bitner, Waltonville. Miss Louise Atkinson, Salem, secured the manuscript for me.

4. Obtained from Mr. Dave H. Adamson, Jr., Belleville, who got it from his mother, Mrs. D. H. Adamson, Sr., Belleville.

5. Communicated by Mr. Dave H. Adamson, Jr., Belleville, who got it from his mother, Mrs. D. H. Adamson, Sr., Belleville.

6. Secured from Mr. Dave H. Adamson, Jr., Belleville, who learned it from his mother, Mrs. D. H. Adamson, Sr., Belleville.

7. Obtained through the courtesy of Mr. William H. Creed of Belleville, from the manuscript book of Mrs. Clara Walpert, of Belleville.

8. Secured from Miss Rosalie Comment, Belleville, who got it from Mrs. Cruikshank, Edgemont Station, Belleville.

9. Obtained from Miss Irene Mache, Belleville, who wrote it down from the singing of Mrs. Schifferdedker, Belleville.

CHAPTER VIII

LOVE IN SENTIMENTAL VERSE

WIDELY popular at one time in Egypt, but now seldom sung, were sentimental love-songs. As it is pictured in these songs, love is seldom joyous and happy, but bowed down with a burden of grief and doubt. These songs lay bare the souls of those bereaved by death and of those jilted by fickle lovers; they tell of young love crossed by the will of parents and separated by prison walls. They raise the question of the permanence of love and grieve over pleasures that are gone.

Somewhat rarely humor creeps into these songs, by way of relief from so much sadness, and sometimes love, most unexpectedly, is a matter of joy and delight. But such songs are uncommon, for love in local folk-songs is a matter for tears, not laughter.

48

KITTY WELLS

Compare Pound, no. 94 and Cox, no. 127. According to Cox, the song is ascribed to Thomas Sloan, Jr.

A¹

You ask what makes this darky weep,
Why he, like others, am not gay,
What makes the tears flow down his cheek
From early morn till close of day.

My story, darkies, you shall hear
While in my memory fresh it dwells
And cause you all to shed a tear
On the grave of my sweet Kitty Wells.

Chorus:

And the birds were singing in the morning,
And the myrtle and the ivy were in bloom,
And the sun o'er the hills it was dawning;
It was then we laid her in her tomb.

I never shall forget the day
That we together roamed the hills;
I kissed her cheek and named the day
That I would marry Kitty Wells.

But death came in my cabin door
And took from me my joy and pride,
And when I found she was no more,
I laid my banjo down and cried.

B²

You ask what makes this darkey weep,
Why he, like others, am not gay,
What makes the tears roll down his cheeks
From early morn to close of day.

Chorus:

Still the birds are singing in the morning,
The myrtle and the ivy are in bloom;
The sun on the hill tops is adorning,
It was there we laid her in the tomb.

My story, darkies, you will hear,
For in my memory fresh it dwells;
It will cause you all to drop a tear
On the grave of my sweet Kitty Wells.

The springtime has not charms for me,
The flowers are blooming in the dells;
There is one sweet form I do not see,
'Tis the form of my sweet Kitty Wells.

I never will forget the day
That we together roamed the dells;
I kissed her cheek and named the day
That I might marry Kitty Wells.

But death came in my cabin door
And took from me my joy and pride,
And when I found she was no more,
Then I laid my banjo down and cried.

Sometimes I wish that I were dead
And laid beside her in her tomb;
The sorrow that bows down my head
'Tis silent in the midnight gloom.

49

THE WIDOW BY THE SEA[3]

Probably this was a popular song of its day, but in Egypt it has become a part of the oral tradition. I can remember hearing my mother sing parts of it; I can recall the tune to which she sang it and a part of the words of the chorus.

Just one year ago tonight, love,
I became your happy bride;
I changed my mansion for a cottage
To dwell with you by the sea.

Chorus:

All alone, alone, you've left me,
And no other's bride I'll be,
For tonight, love, I'm a widow
In my cottage by the sea.

In my cottage by the seaside
I can see my mansion home
O'er the hills and through the valley
Even where I used to roam.

Oh, you told me I'd be happy,
And no happiness I see,
In the bridal flowers you decked me
In my cottage by the sea.

Oh, my poor and aged father,
How he'd weep and mourn and cry!
And my poor and aged mother
How the tears for me would flow!

Oh, my one and only brother,
How he'd weep and mourn and cry,
Just to know that I'm a widow
In my cottage by the sea.

50

LITTLE NELL[4]

The correct title of this song is "Bright-Eyed Little
Nell of Narragansett Bay." At one time it was a popular song. Spaeth, *Weep Some More, My Lady*, pp. 30–31,
gives the words and music of it.

How well do I remember those boyhood happy hours,
The cottage in the garden where grew the fairest
    flowers,
The bright and sparkling water o'er which we loved to
    sail
With hearts so gay for miles away o'er the gentle gale.

I loved this little beauty; my boat it was my pride;
With her close beside me we loved to roam the tide.
She laughed in glee so merrily to see the waves go by.
How loudly was the wind that blew and merry was the
    sky!

The thunder rolled around us; the nights were dark and
    drear.
We loved to roam the ocean without a thought of fear.
Lightning flashed around us and darted through the
    sky
O'er bright-eyed laughing little Nell of Narrangansett
    Bay.

One day she strolled away from us and soon was in the
    boat;
The cord was quickly loosened, and with the tide afloat
The treacherous bark blew lightly and fast before the
    wind;
Soon friends and home and all that was dear was many
    miles behind.

Next day her lifeless body was cast upon the beach;
I stood and gazed upon it bereaved of sense of speech;
It's years since we parted, but eer (ere) I weep today
O'er bright-eyed little laughing Nell of Narrangansett
    Bay.

Tolled, tolled, the bell from early dawn till day;
Lovely Nell so quickly passed away.
Tolled, tolled the bell so sad and mournfully
O'er bright-eyed little laughing Nell of Narrangansett
    Bay.

51

WEEPING WILLOW

    The first variant of this song has the title, "Weeping
Willow," the second "Weeping Willow Tree." Sandburg (*The American Songbag*, p. 314) says that the song
is sung in all the states and that it is an old one.

    For comparison of texts see Fuson, *Ballads of the
Kentucky Highlands*, p. 126, and Sandburg, *The American Songbag*, pp. 314 f.

A[5]

My heart is broken with grief and sorrow,
Grieving for the one I love,
But still I know that I will never see him,
Till we meet in heaven above.

Chorus:

Bury me beneath the willow,
Beneath the weeping willow tree,
And when he knows where I've been sleeping,
Then perhaps he'll think of me.

He told me that he always loved me.
How could I think him untrue,
Until an angel softly whispered,
"He was untrue to you?"

Next Sunday was her wedding day,
But God only knows where he may be,
. . . .
And he cares no more for me.

B[6]

My heart is broken; I'm in sorrow
O'er the one I love,
But still I know I'll never see him,
Till we meet in heaven above.

Chorus:

Then bury me beneath the weeping tree,
Beneath the weeping, the weeping willow tree,
That he may know where I am sleeping,
And perhaps he'll weep for me.

He told me that he didn't love me,
But how could I believe him true
Until my guardian angel told me,
"He will prove untrue to you."

Tomorrow was our wedding day.
Oh, God! Where can he be?
He's gone away to wed another
And no longer cares for me.

52

THE BROKEN HEART[7]

Fuson, *Ballads of the Kentucky Highlands*, p. 140,
prints this song under the title, "Broken Vows." Except for a number of verbal changes, his version resembles closely the Southern Illinois variant.

Would have been better for us both
Had we never in this wide, wicked world to have met,
Though the pleasures we've both seen together,
I shall never, no never, forget.

Chorus:

Oh, how sadly my heart turns toward you;
Though the distant have thrown us apart,
Do you love me as dear as when you pressed me
On your bosom so near to your heart?

Would have been better for us both to remained
strangers,
Though why should I speak of it now,
For long, long have I felt the danger
Of a heart broken through a false vow.

Oh, you told me you always would love me,
And nothing should ever come between;
It's been long, long ago since you told me,
But those words on my memory still cling.

Oh, all my hopes have departed,
But I'll try and struggle through this vain world,
And if ever I die broken-hearted,
I'll employ your name to be my last words.

Oh, remember when the cold grave's around me;
Will you come, love, and drop a single tear
And tell to the strangers all around you
That a heart you have broken lies here?

53

THE LITTLE ROSEWOOD CASKET[8]

See Spaeth, *Weep Some More, My Lady*, p. 35. The
Southern Illinois variant has more stanzas than the one
that Spaeth has included in his collection.

There's a little rosewood casket,
Sitting on a marble stand.
There's a package of love letters,
Written by my true love's hand.

So (when) dreams in view me, brother,
Come sit upon my bed,
Lay my aching head on a pillow
While my aching heart grows dead.

In that little rosewood casket
That is resting on the stand,
Lies a package of old love letters
Written by a true love's hand.

You may go and get them, brother,
And sit down there by my bed,
And press gently to your bosom
This poor aching, throbbing head.

You have brought them to me, brother,
You may read them now to me,
I have often tried to read them
But for tears I could not see.

Last Sunday night I saw him walking
With a lady by his side,
And I thought I heard him whisper
I could never be his bride.

When I am dead and in my coffin,
And my friends all gather round,
And my narrow grave is ready
In some lonesome church yard ground;

Take this package of old letters,
Fold them all around my heart
And this little ring he gave me
From my finger never part.

54

I HAVE FINISHED HIM A LETTER[9]

This song seems to have enjoyed some little popularity with the young people forty years or more ago. Today it is rarely sung. This particular version was copied from a manuscript written many years ago.

I have finished him the letter
To tell him he is free
From this moment and forever
He's nothing more to me.
And my heart feels like the gayest
When at last the deed is done;
It will teach him when he's courting
He should never court but one.

Everybody in the village
Knows that he's been courting me,
And this morning he was riding
With his saucy Anna Lee,
And they say he smiled upon her
As he glided by her side.
I've no doubt he's made her promise
That some day she'll be his bride.

It was twilight in the evening
When he said he would call on me,
But perhaps he is with Miss Anna;
He may stay there, too, for me.
Just as sure as I am living
If he ever comes more,
I will act as if we never,
Never, never, met before.

I have finished him a letter
To tell him he is free;
He may have her if he wants her
If he loves her more than me.
Let him go; it will not kill me;
I will say the same; so there!
If I knew it was forever,
It would be more than I could bear.

I declare out in the twilight
There is some one coming now;
Could it be him? 'tis his figure;
Just as sure as I am here
There is some one at the gate now;
I will meet him at the door;
I will tell him he is welcome
If he courts Miss Lee no more.

Everybody knows I've been wooing
And they know I've wooed in vain;
If he can live happy with another
Never think of me again,
And to you it is a pleasure,
And to me it is a pain;
For the loss of such a treasure
Never to win those smiles again.

55

TO MEET AGAIN[10]

"To Meet Again" also was copied from a manuscript written years ago. One suspects that it owes something to the vogue of "Nobody's Darling."

I sit broken-hearted tonight, love,
A-thinking of you, darling one,
Of days that have passed and never to come;
My pleasures forever are gone.

Chorus:
There's no one to kiss me good night, love;
There is no one to care for me now;
There's no one to brush back the golden curls;
There's no hand to lay on my brow.

Last night in my dreams I could see you;
Your face looked as bright and as fair
As the night we parted forever;
In waking I found you not there.

But when I am awake, I am thinking
How you prest me so close to your heart
And whispered, "God knows that I love you,
But, Darling, we have to part."

You promised you would remember
The one that has been faithful to thee;
You brushed the hair from my temples
And whispered, "Don't grieve after me."

You kissed me good night and you left me
A-watching you out of my sight;
I whispered to heaven and murmured,
"I am no one's darling tonight."

I promised some day I would meet you
In the happy bright home in the sky;
There there will be no more parting;
We'll never say good-bye.

56

GOOD NIGHT, BYE-BYE, FOREVER[11]

Inconstant love is the theme of this song, which appears to be well on the road to oblivion.

This night we part forever;
You are nothing more to me;
You have broken my heart for another;
Not a tear would I shed for thee.

Chorus:

Good night, bye, bye, forever;
You are nothing more to me;
You have broken my heart for another;
Not a tear would I shed for thee.

Take back the ring you gave me;
It was once so dear to me;
Go give it to another;
It is nothing more to me.

Go break the heart of another
As you have broken mine.
Go tell her that you love her
And be forever thine.

You once sought me as an ideal;
You were all the world to me;
You cast me off for another;
Not a tear would I shed for thee.

Yes, I hope that God's sweet blessings
May forever rest on thee,
And you'll never treat another
As you have treated me.

57

I'M THINE OVER THE LEFT[12]

This song is perhaps the work of some poetaster, moved to composition by the reading of Burns. What the significance of the phrase "over the left" may be I do not know.

Like a number of other songs in this chapter, "I'm Thine Over the Left" owes its survival in Southern Illinois to the fact that it was written down in a manuscript book.

I'm thine in my gladness, I'm thine in my tears.
My love it can change not with absence of years;
My love it can change not with absence of years.

Were a dungeon thy dwelling my home it would be,
For its gloom would be sunshine if I were with thee;
For its gloom would be sunshine if I were with thee.

But life has no beauty since of thee I'm bereft;
I'm thine and thine only, I'm thine over the left;
Thine and thine only, over the left.

58

WHY DID YOU GO?[13]
OR
BLUE DAYS

You make me sad, you make me glad,
You make me feel so blue;
You make the blue sky gray.
You drove the sunshine away.

Chorus:
You make the blue sky gray,
You drive the sunshine away;
You are the only one today
Can drive the blue days away.

You have broken all of your vows,
But I still love you somehow.
You're the only one today
That can drive my blue days away.

Why did you say when you went away
That you'd never return?
I missed you so! Why did you go,
If you knew how I've yearned!

59

OLD SMOKY MOUNTAIN[14]

There is evidence of confusion in this song; the second, third, and fourth stanzas (the latter two only remembered in part) appear to be taken from "A Forsaken Lover."[15]

Compare with Fuson, *Ballads of the Kentucky Highlands*, pp. 119–120.

On top of old Smoky,
The mountain so high,
Where the wild birds and turtle doves
Can hear my sad cry,

Sparking is a pleasure,
And parting is a grief,
But a false-hearted lover
Is worse than a thief.

A thief can but rob you,

. . . .

But a false-hearted lover
Will take you to your grave.

. . . .

. . . .

For there isn't one girl in twenty
That a poor boy can trust.

Go put up your horses
And give them some hay;
Come sit beside me
As long as you stay.

My wagon is loaded,
On rolling away;
So farewell, my darling;
I'll speed on my way.

Your parents are against me,
And mine are the same;
If I'm down on your books, love,
Please rub off my name.

On top of Old Smoky,
The mountain so high,
Where the wild birds and turtle dove
Can hear my sad cry.

As soon as the dew drops
Fall upon the green lawn,
Last night she was with me,
But now she is gone.

I can love little,
Or I can love long,
Or I can love an old sweetheart
Until a new one comes along.

60

BROKEN-HEARTED[16]

They have given you to another;
They have broken every vow;
They have given you to another;
My heart is lonely now.

They remembered not our parting;
They remembered not our tears;
They severed in one moment
The happiness of years.

But gold I know hath won thee,
Thy touching heart beguile;
Your mother too does shun me,
For she knows I love her chile.

You know you have spoken words
I never can forget;
Although I'm broken-hearted,
I love you, love you yet.

They have given you to another;
You love him too, they say.
If memory hath not changed thee,
Perhaps, perhaps it may.

They have given thee to another;
Thou art now his gentle bride.
Had I loved you as a brother,
I could see you by his side.

61

MOONLIGHT, ALONE[17]

This song is known in other sections as "Moonlight",
"Meet Me in the Moonlight," (and as "The Prisoner's
Song."—J.W.A.)
See Sandburg, *The American Songbag*, pp. 216–217,
and Fuson, *Ballads of the Kentucky Highlands*, p. 143.

I am going to the new jail tomorrow,
Leaving such a loved one behind,
With the cold iron bars all around me
And a stone for a pillow I find.

Chorus:

Oh meet me, oh meet me tonight, love,
Oh, meet me by the moonlight alone,
For I have a sad story to tell you,
Must be told by the moonlight alone.

Oh, I have a large ship on the ocean
All lined in with silver and gold,
And before my loved one shall suffer
That ship shall be anchored and sold.

Oh, I know that your parents just hate me
And would drive me away from the door,
And if I had my life to live over
I would never go there any more.

Oh, I wish I had some one to love me,
Some one who would call me his own,
Some one who would stay with me always,
For I'm tired of living alone.

It was only last night I was dreaming
Of the one that I loved long ago,
And the bright light from his eyes that come
    beaming
As he whispered so softly and low.

62

THE MAPLE ON THE HILL[18]

This song seems to owe its survival to the fact that
it was written down, for no one sings it in Egypt today.

Near a quiet country village grew a maple on the hill;
There I sat with my Genettie long ago;
The stars were shining brightly and we heard the
    whippoorwill
When we sat beneath the maple on the hill.

Oh, I'm growing old and feeble and the stars are shining
    bright;
Will you listen to the murmuring of the rill?
Will you fold your arms around me as you did the
    stormy night
When we sat beneath the maple on the hill?

We would sing love songs together when the birds had
    gone to rest;
Will you listen to the murmuring of the rill?
Will you fold your arms around me, place your hands
    upon my breast
As you did the stormy night when we sat beneath the
    maple on the hill?

Don't forget me, little darling, when I am laid beneath
the sod;
There's one more wish, my darling, that I crave:
Will you linger there in silence when my spirit's with
the dead?
Will your teardrops sweeten the flowers on my grave?

Chorus:

Oh, I'll soon be with the angels on that bright and
happy shore.
Even now I hear them singing over the rill.
Will you always love me, darling? I must leave you; I
must go.
I will leave you with the maple on the hill.

63[19]

WILL YOU LOVE ME WHEN I AM OLD?

This song was also preserved in manuscript.

I ask of you, my darling, a question soft and low;
It (true) gives me many a heart-ache as the moments
come and go;
Your love, she may be truthful, but the truest of love
grows cold,
And it's only this, my darling, will you love me when I
am old?

Chorus:

Life's morns shall soon be waneing,
And the evening bells be tolled,
And my heart shall know no sadness
If you'll love me when I'm old.

Down the stream of life together we are sailing side by
  side,
Hoping some bright day to anchor safe beyond the
  sunny tide;
Today the skies are cloudless, but tonight many clouds
  unfold,
And the storm may gather around us if you'll love me
  when I'm old.

My hair shall shine as snowdrifts and my eyes shall
  dimmer grow
As I'll lean upon some loved one in the valley as I
  strown. [?]
Then I'd claim of you a promise worth to me a world of
  gold,
And it's only this, my darling, will you love me when
  I'm old?

64

THE OLD OAKEN TREE[20]

Unlike most of the songs in this chapter, "The Old
Oaken Tree" is happy, though old-fashioned to modern
ears and a trifle cloying in sentiment. It sounds like a
one-time popular song.

    Beautiful miss, fair little maid,
    Maiden with soft golden hair,
    Each evening she meets me with one loving,
    Loving kiss over the echo of love.

Chorus:
Down by the lane and over the stiles,
Under the old oken tree,
The clock strikes nine; the starres brightly
  shine;
There's some body waiting for me,

Her eyes is like dimonds or the stars in the sky;
Her hair was a beautiful brown;
Each evening she meets me with one loving
    (kiss);
Sirs, listen, I'll tell you where.

65

MY HORSES AIN'T HUNGRY[21]

For a discussion of this song see Cox, *Folk-Songs of the South*, p. 433.

One stanza of this song appears with verbal changes in "Farewell, Sweet Mary," Cox, no. 146—stanza one —and also in "Jack O' Diamonds," Lomax, *Cowboy Songs*, p. 292.

> My horses ain't hungry;
> They won't eat your hay;
> So fare you will, Polly;
> I'm going away.
>
> Your parents don't like me;
> They say I'm too poor;
> They say I'm not worthy
> To enter your door.
>
> I know they don't like,
> But why do you care?
> You know I'm your, Polly;
> You know I'm your dear.
>
> I know you're my Polly,
> But I've not long to stay;
> So go with me, darling;
> We'll speed on our way.

Yes, I will go with you;
You're poor, I am told;
It's your love I'm wanting,
Not silver and gold.

We'll load our belongings;
We'll drive till we come
To some little cabin;
We'll call it our home.

I hate to leave Mama;
She treats me so kind,
But I'll go as I promised
That Johnny of mine;

So good-bye, dear Mama;
I'm leaving today;
We'll journey on farther
And speed on our way.

66

JACK AND JOE[22]
OR
JACK AND NELL

Three years ago since Jack and Joe
Set sail across the foam;
Each vowed a fortune he would gain
Before returning home.

Chorus:

"Give my love to Nellie, Jack,
And kiss her once for me.
The sweetest girl in all this world
I am sure you'll say is she.

Treat her kindly, Jack old pal,
And tell her I am well."
His parting words were
"Don't forget to give my love to Nell."

In one short year Jack gained his wealth
And started home the (that) day,
But when the pals shook hands to part,
Poor Joe could only say:

Three years had passed when Joe at last
Gained wealth enough for life.
He started home across the foam
To make sweet Nell his wife.

But when he learned that Jack and Nell
One year ago had wed,
With sobs and threats he now regrets
That he had ever said:

They chanced to meet upon the street;
Joe said, "You selfish elf,
The very next girl I learn to love
I'll kiss her for myself."

But all is fair in love, they say.
Since you have gone and wed,
I'll not be angry with you pal;
So once again I say:

Chorus:

NOTES ON CHAPTER VIII

1. Copied from the singing of Mrs. Charles Neely, Sr., Carbondale.
2. Obtained from Mr. Dave H. Adamson, Belleville.
3. Copied from a manuscript belonging to Mrs. Hattie Bitner, Waltonville. The manuscript was obtained through the courtesy of Miss Louise Atkinson, Salem.
4. Secured from Mr. Fred Kirby, Flora. He learned this song from his mother.
5. Obtained from Miss Hallie Eubanks, Belleville.

6. Written down for me by Miss Inez Watson, Carterville. This is one of the songs in the Watson-James manuscript book.

7. Through the courtesy of Miss Louise Atkinson, Salem, copied from a manuscript belonging to Mrs. Hattie Bitner, Waltonville.

8. Copied from the manuscript book belonging to the Watson and James families of Carterville.

9. Secured, through the courtesy of Miss Louise Atkinson, Salem, Ill., from a manuscript belonging to Mrs. Hattie Bitner, Waltonville.

10. Copied from a manuscript belonging to Mrs. Hattie Bitner of Waltonville.

11. Copied from a manuscript belonging to Mrs. Hattie Bitner, Waltonville.

12. Through the courtesy of Mr. William H. Creed, copied from the manuscript book of Mrs. Clara Walpert, Belleville.

13. Obtained from Miss Hallie M. Eubanks, Belleville.

14. Obtained from Miss Hallie M. Eubanks, Belleville.

15.

"O meeting is a pleasure,
But to part with him was grief;
But an unconstant true lover
Is worse than a thief.

A thief can but rob you
And take all you have;
But an unconstant lover
Will take you to your grave.

The grave it will rot you
And turn you to dust;
There is scarce one out of twenty
That a young girl can trust."

Cox, *Folk-Songs of the South*, p. 425.

16. Through the courtesy of Mr. William H. Creed, Belleville, copied from the manuscript book of Mrs. Clara Walpert, Belleville.

17. Through the courtesy of Miss Louise Atkinson, Salem, copied from a manuscript belonging to Mrs. Hattie Bitner, Waltonville.

18. Through the courtesy of Miss Louise Atkinson, Salem, copied from a manuscript that belongs to Mrs. Hattie Bitner, Waltonville.

19. Copied from a manuscript of Mrs. Hattie Bitner, Waltonville, through the courtesy of Miss Louise Atkinson, Salem.

20. From a manuscript of Mrs. Hattie Bitner, which I secured through the courtesy of Miss Louise Atkinson, Salem.

21. Obtained from Miss Emilie Huck, New Baden.

22. Secured from Miss Hallie M. Eubanks, Belleville.

CHAPTER IX

CHILDHOOD AND TEMPERANCE

CHILDHOOD fares no better than love in local folk-songs, for it is painted for us by sentimental writers of modest talent and little understanding of children. In fact, it seems not to have been the intent of the writer to give us an insight into the childish emotion but to wring as many tears as possible with a morbid play upon sentiment. We are invited, in superficial verse, to grieve over the bereavement of children, often thrown upon the mercies of a cold and harsh world; we are invited to shed tears over deathbed scenes and to share the sorrow of children deserted by erring parents. With love and childhood pictured in such dismal colors, one is led to suspect that the world must indeed have seemed but a vale of tears to many people of a past generation.

These poetasters of sentimental turn also did effective yeoman service to the cause of temperance. By means of children and wives they struck many a blow (under the belt, it seems at times) at demon rum. These temperance-songs are of a piece with *Ten Nights in a Barroom* and *The Drunkard*.

67

THE BLIND ORPHAN[1]

Fuson, *Ballads of the Kentucky Highlands*, p. 146, prints a fragmentary variant of this song.

> They say, dear father, that tonight
> You will wed another bride,
> That you will clasp her in your arms
> Where my dear mother died;

That she will lean her graceful head
Upon your loving breast
Where she who now lies low in death
In her last hours did rest.

They say her name is Mary, too,
The name my mother bore.
Dear father, is she kind and true
Like the one you loved before?

And is her step so soft and low,
Her voice so sweet and mild?
Dear father, will she love me, too,
Your blind and helpless child?

Please, father, do not bid me come
To meet your new-made bride,
For I could not greet her in the room
Where my dear mother died.

Her picture is hanging on the wall;
Her books are lying near,
And there the harp her fingers touched,
And there is her vacant chair.

The chair where by I used to kneel
To say my evening prayer.
Dear father, it would break my heart;
I could not meet her there.

And when I cry myself to sleep,
As now I often do,
And softly to my chamber creep
My new mama and you

Then bid her gently press a kiss
Upon my throbbing brow,
Just as my own dear mother did;
Papa, you are weeping now.

I know I love you, Papa dear,
But how I long to go
Where God is light and I am sure
There will be no blind ones there.

Now, let me kneel down by your side
And to our dear Savior pray
That God's right hand may find you both
Up life's long weary way.

The prayer was offered and a song.
"I am weary, now," she said.
Her father raised her in his arms
And laid her on the bed.

And as he turned to leave the room
One joyful cry was given.
He turned and caught the last sweet smile;
His blind child was in heaven.

They buried her by her mother's side
And raised a marble flare;
On it inscribed the simple words,
"There will be no blind ones there."

68

BAGGAGE COACH AHEAD[2]

Written by Gussie Davis and based upon an actual event,[3] this song owes much of its popularity to the fact that it was sung on vaudeville circuits and illustrated by colored pictures thrown upon the screen.[4]

See Pound, no. 58, and Spaeth, *Weep Some More, My Lady*, p. 242.

On a dark stormy night as the train rattled on
All passengers had gone to bed,
Except one young man with a babe in his arms,
Who sat with a bowed-down head.
Just then the babe began to cry,
As if its poor heart would break.
"Take it out," said a man. "Don't keep it in here.
We paid for our berths and want rest."
But not a word from the man with the babe,
As he sat with it close to his breast.
"Oh, where is its mother? Go take it to her,"
A lady then softly said.
"I wish that I could" was the man's reply,
"But she is dead in the coach ahead."
As the train rolled onward a husband sat in tears,
Thinking of the happiness of future years.
Baby's face brings pictures of some cherished hope
That stands, for baby's cry can't waken her
In the baggage coach ahead.

69

HELLO CENTRAL, GIVE ME HEAVEN[5]

Charles K. Harris composed this piece, which started
a craze for telephone songs, according to Spaeth.[6] (It
was used for "illustrated songs" during the early days
of the motion picture.—J.W.A.)

Compare Spaeth, *Weep Some More, My Lady*,
pp. 250–251.

"Papa, I'm so sad and lonely,"
Sobbed a tearful little child;
"Since dear Mamma went to heaven,
Papa, darling, you've not smiled.

I will speak to her and tell her
That we want her to come home;
Just you listen and I'll call her
Through the telephone."

Chorus:

"Hello, Central! give me heaven,
For my Mamma's there.
You can find her with the angels
On the golden stair;

She'll be glad it's me who's speaking;
Call her, won't you, please?
For I want to surely tell her
We're so lonely here."

When the girl received this message
O'er the telephone,
How her heart thrilled in that moment,
And the wires seemed to moan,

"I will answer, just to please her;
Yes, dear heart, I'll soon be home."
"Kiss me, Mamma, kiss your darling
Through the telephone."

70

OH, WHAT I'D GIVE FOR A MOTHER[7]

An old man was seated one evening
In an easy chair close by the fire;
The little child standing beside him
Was a picture of health to admire.

"Please tell me, dear Grandpa, of mother;
Her sweet face I never shall see,
Although in my dreams I've beheld her
So tenderly smiling at me.

Chorus:

"Oh, what would I give for a mother
To teach me the way I should go!
Oh, what would I give for a mother
Dear Grandpa, I long for her so;

Had I all this world's richest treasures
With gold and with jewels in store,
I'd gladly give all for a mother
And never be sad any more.

"My mother, they say, was a victim
Of fate that was hard to recall."
"Yes, child," said the old man,
"She married a man that was loved by us all;

She kissed him goodbye one sad morning.
For him we have searched, but in vain;
Your mother soon died broken-hearted."
With grief the poor child cried again.

71

NOBODY'S DARLING[8]

Compare the text with Spaeth, *Weep Some More,
My Lady*, pp. 21–22.

Out in the cold world alone.
Walking about in the street,
Asking a penny for bread;
Begging from each one I meet,
Barelegs and friendless and cold,
Nothing but sorrow I see,
For I am nobody's darling;
Nobody cares for me.

Chorus:

Nobody's darling on earth;
Heaven will merciful be,
For I am nobody's darling;
Nobody cares for me.
No one to kiss me good-night;
No one to ease my poor head;
Up in the attic at night,
Weeping for those who are dead,
Chilling wind chilling my brow,
Sitting on poverty's knee,
For I am nobody's darling;
Nobody cares for me.

Oft times at night as I kneel,
Lifting my sorrowful eye,
Asking a mother to smile
Down on a child from the sky,
Then I'll forget all of my grief;
Mother in heaven I see,
For then I'll be somebody's darling;
Somebody cares for me.

Chorus:

Nobody's darling on earth;
Heaven will merciful be,
For then I shall be somebody's darling;
Somebody cares for me.

72

POOR LITTLE JOE[9]

See Cox, no. 152.

While strolling one night through New York's busy
    throng
I met a poor boy; he was singing a song.
Although he was smiling he wanted for bread,
And though he was singing he wished himself dead.

Cold blew the wind and down came the snow;
He'd nowhere to shelter and no place to go;
No mother to guide him, in the grave she's laid low.
Cast out on this wide world was poor little Joe.

A carriage passed by with a lady inside;
She looked on poor Joe's face and saw that he cried.
He followed the carriage; she not even smiled
But fondly caressed her own darling child.

73

PUT ME IN MY LITTLE BED[10]

The writer of this piece uses the same technique that
is employed in "Let Me Say My Little Prayer" and
"Put My Little Shoes Away."

O, birdie, I am tired now; I do not care to hear you
    sing.
You have sung your happy song all day; now put your
    head beneath your wing.
I'm sleepy, too, as I can be; but, sister, when your
    prayers are said,
I want to lay me down to sleep; so put me in my little
    bed.

O Birdie, I Am Tired Now

VERSE

O bird - ie, I am ti - red now, I do not

care to hear you sing; You have sung your hap - py song all

day; Now put your head be-neath your wing; I am sleep - y

too, as I can be. . . But, sis - ter, when your prayers are

said, I want to lay me down to sleep, So put me

CHORUS

in my lit - tle bed. Come, sis - ter, come, kiss me good-

night, For I my eve-ning prayer have said, I am ti - red

now and sleep-y, too, So put me in my lit - tle bed.

Chorus:

Come, sister, come kiss me good night, for I my eve-
    ning prayer have said.
I'm tired now and sleepy, too, so put me in my little bed.

Oh, sister, what did mother say when to heaven was
    called away?
She told me always to be good and never, never go
    astray.
I can't forget the day she died; she placed her hand
    upon my head;
She whispered softly, "My child," and then they told
    me she was dead.

Dear sister, come and hear my prayer now ere I lay
    me down to sleep,
Within my heavenly Father's care, while angels bright
    their vigils keep,
And let me ask of him above to keep my soul in paths
    of right;
Oh, let me thank Him for His love ere I shall say my
    last goodnight.

B[11]

SONG BALET OF BIRDY

Oh, Byrday, I am tired now;
I do not care to heare you sing.
You have sung your happy songs all day;
Now put your head beneath your wing.

I am tired, too, as I can be.
And, Sister, when my prayr I've sed
I want to lay me down to sleep;
So put me in my little bed.

Chorus:

Come, sister, come, kiss me goodnight,
For I've my eavening prayar have sed.
I am tired now and sleepy, too,
So put me in my little bed.

Dear Sister, what did mother say
When she was called to heaven away?
She told me allways to be good
And never, never go astray.

I can't forget the day she died;
She placed hir hand uppond my head,
She whispered softly, "Keep my child,"
And then they told me she was dead.

74

PUT MY LITTLE SHOES AWAY[12]

See Spaeth, *Weep Some More, My Lady*, pp. 25–26.

Mother dear, come bathe my forehead,
For I am growing weak.
Let one little drop of water fall
Upon my burning cheek.
Tell my loving little schoolmates
That I never more will play;
Give them all my toys, Mother;
Put my little shoes away.

Chorus:

I am growing tired, Mother;
Soon I'll say to all, good day.
You will don't (not) forget, dearest Mother;
Put my little shoes away.

Santa Claus, they gave them to me
With a lot of other things,
And I think he brought an angel
With a pair of golden wings.
Mother, I'll be an angel by perhaps another day.
You will don't forget, dearest Mother;
Put my little shoes away.

Soon the baby will be larger,
And they'll fit his little feet.
O, he looks so nice and cunning
As he walks along the street.
I'm getting weaker, Mother;
Soon I'll say to all good day.
Please remember what I tell you;
Put my little shoes away.

75

PAGE FROM THE SCRAP-BOOK OF LIFE[13]

I stood in the glare of the city
And gazed on the passing throng,
As, wrapped in their joys and sorrow,
They jostled and hurried along.
While there in the crowd, came a woman
In satin and jewel array.
It seems I could trace upon her sad face
A tale of a happier day.

Chorus:

'Tis a page from the scrap-book of life;
'Tis a story that never grows old;
'Tis the tale of a once happy wife,
Who like others was tempted by gold.
'Tis a story that's too sad to tell
Of a world and its battle and strife;
'Tis a page from life's history, blotted with tears;
'Tis a page from the scrap-book of life.

In a little house in the country
A sad-hearted father still waits,
While a little tot for her mother,
Close down by the old garden gate.
"Oh, please, sir, have you seen my mamma?"
She asked of each one passing by.
"If you see her, won't you please tell her
To come back to Daddy and I?"

76

THE DRUNKARD'S LONE CHILD[14]

The local title of this song is "Song Ballet of a Drunkard's Child."

Compare with Spaeth, *Weep Some More, My Lady*, pp. 191–192.

Out in this dreary night sadly I roam;
I have no mother, no friend, and no home;
Nobody cares for me, no one should cry
Even if poor little Bessie should die.

Mother, oh why did you leave me alone;
No one to love me, no one to care;
Dark is the night and the storm was wild;
God pity Bessie, the drunkard's lone child.

Barefooted and cold I've wandered all day,
Asking for work, but I'm too young, they say;
All day long I've been beggin' for bread;
Father's a drunkard and mother is dead.

We were so happy till Father drunk rum;
Then all our troubles began;
Mother grew weak as she wept each day;
Baby and I were too hungry to play.

Slowly they faded till one summer night
Found her sweet face all silent and white;
Then with big tears all rolling and falling I said,
"Father's a drunkard and mother is dead."

The Drunkard's Lone Child

Bare-foot'd and cold   I've wan-dered all day,   Ask-ing for

work, but I'm too young, they say;   All   day long I've been

beg-ging for bread, Fa-ther's a drunk-ard, and moth-er is dead.

Moth-er, oh, why   did you leave me a-lone!   No one to

love me,   no one to care;   Dark   is the night, and the

storm was wild;   God   pit-y   Bes-sie, the drunkard's lone child.

If some men of temperance only could find
Poor dear father and speak very kind;
If they could keep him from drinking, why then
We would be very happy again.

Men of temperance, please try
Or poor little Bessie will soon starve and die;
Down on this damp ground I must lay my head;
Father's a drunkard and mother is dead.

77

THE DRUNKARD'S WIFE[15]

This piece is known locally as "Don't Go Out To-night." Compare with Fuson, *Ballads of the Kentucky Highlands*, p. 137.

Don't go out tonight, my darling;
Do not leave me here alone;
Stay at home tonight, my darling;
I am lonely when you're gone.

Though the wine cup may be tempting
And your friends are full of glee,
I will do my best to cheer you.
Darling, won't you stay with me?

Chorus:

Don't go out tonight, my darling;
Do not leave me here alone;
Stay at home tonight, my darling;
I am lonely when you're gone.

Don't go out tonight, my darling,
For my heart is filled with fear;
Stay at home tonight, my darling;
Let me feel your presence near.

O, my God, he's gone and left me
With the curse upon his lips.
Who can tell how much I've suffered
From the dreaded cup he drank?

Hear the tread of heavy footsteps;
Hear the knock upon the door;
They have brought me home my husband;
There he lies upon the floor.

No caress of mine can wake him;
All he craves is rum, more rum,
And the fondest hopes I've cherished
All have vanished one by one.

NOTES ON CHAPTER IX

1. Through the courtesy of Miss Louise Atkinson, Salem. Copied from a manuscript which belongs to Mrs. Hattie Bitner of Waltonville.

2. Obtained from Miss Hallie M. Eubanks, Belleville.

3. Spaeth, *Read 'Em and Weep*, p. 174.

4. Pound, *American Ballads and Songs*, p. 250.

5. Copied, through the courtesy of Miss Louise Atkinson, Salem, from a manuscript belonging to Mrs. Hattie Bitner, Waltonville.

6. Spaeth, *Weep Some More, My Lady*, p. 250.

7. Copied from a manuscript belonging to Mrs. Hattie Bitner, Waltonville, which was secured through the courtesy of Miss Louise Atkinson, Salem.

8. Through the courtesy of Miss Louise Atkinson, Salem. This piece was copied from a manuscript of Mrs. Hattie Bitner, Waltonville.

9. Secured from Miss Irene Mache, Belleville.

10. Copied, through the courtesy of Mr. William H. Creed, from the manuscript book of Mrs. Clara Walpert, Belleville.

11. Copied from a manuscript of Mrs. Hattie Bitner, Waltonville, through the courtesy of Miss Louise Atkinson.

12. Obtained from the manuscript book of Mrs. Clara Walpert, Belleville, through the courtesy of Mr. William H. Creed.

13. Secured from Mr. Fred Kirby, Flora.

14. Through the courtesy of Miss Louise Atkinson, copied from a manuscript of Mrs. Hattie Bitner, Waltonville.

15. Copied from a manuscript of Mrs. Hattie Bitner, Waltonville, through the courtesy of Miss Louise Atkinson.

CHAPTER X

BALLADS AND SONGS OF LOCAL INTEREST

IN A FEW instances, local tragedies and situations have inspired ballads and songs. A convent fire at Belleville and a flood at Shawneetown moved two poetasters to composition, but neither piece gained wide circulation in Egypt. Nor are they very well known in those towns themselves. Interest in the tragedies gave the ballads a passing significance. Today only people of antiquarian interests recall them. The execution of Charlie Burger, the notorious gangster of Shady Rest, in Saline County, called forth a ballad that was perhaps more widely current than either of the other two pieces. But it, too, quickly lost its appeal. A song, possibly of Negro origin, tells how a girl in Cairo put ideas into the head of some man's sweetheart. Although this song may have more merit than the others, there is no evidence that it is generally known.

78

THE BELLEVILLE CONVENT FIRE[1]

Kind friends, give attention to what I relate,
And ever remember those poor children's fate.
In full health and vigor they retired for the night,
Not thinking of fire that raged with its might.
The room and the hallways were clouded with smoke
When the dear little children from slumber awoke.
They rushed to the stairway; it would make brave
        hearts sigh
To see those white faces at the windows so high.

Refrain:

No one to help them, no one to bless,
No one to save them in their sad distress.
It was in Belleville City; sad grief did abound
On the night that the convent was burned to the
ground.

When the loud cry of "Fire" was heard in the air,
Fathers and mothers were seen everywhere.
When the firemen arrived, alas, 'twas too late,
For all in the convent had met their sad fate.
A girl stood at the window, three stories high,
"O, save, me, Dear Mother," in vain did she cry.
Just then an explosion, we grieve to relate,
And all in the convent had met their sad fate.

[Refrain]

Let us mention one pure soul who went with the rest
To the sweet land above to be there ever blest.
The brave Holy Mother from rooms would not go
Although twice before she had been down below.
But like a brave hero she stood to her post
When she was sure that the children would shortly be
lost.
She rushed up the stairway with a fearful cry,
Praying to God with her children to die.
We know they have gone to a far better shore,
Where the death-dealing fire fiend can reach them no
more.
Let us hope we shall meet them up there again
Where there is no sorrow, anguish, or pain.

79

SHAWNEETOWN FLOOD[2]

This ballad celebrates the flood of 1913, which
brought disaster to Shawneetown. When I visited the
town, people pointed out houses that had been dam-

aged and told me a number of stories concerning the flood. One of these stories was about a Negro who recovered the use of his legs after being unable to walk for years. The town is completely surrounded by levees, and when the water broke through, the force of the current upset houses and made escape difficult for those who were caught in the town.

In the town of Shawneetown,
When the evening shades came down,
On a quiet Sabbath evening, cold and gray,
While the people walked the streets,
Some in dear communion sat
Within their peaceful homes at the close of day.

All at once the bells were ringing,
With a wild and awful ring,
As the fearful flood broke over one and all,
Oh! that faithful levee broke,
Pale the lips of those who spoke
While that roaring, crashing, awful flood came in.

There were heroes in that day,
Franklin Robinson, they all say,
In his little boat brought many safe ashore;
While they struggled with the waves,
He rode on their lives to save,
Working bravely till that awful flood was o'er.

Father Bikeman saw it coming,
Like a giant mountain high,
And he knew what awful danger,
In its pathway lie.
Oh! he did his duty well
As he boldly rang the bell,
Warning all within the danger line to fly.

On it came with mighty force,
Spoiling all within its course.
Wrecking homes and snatching loved ones from their
    friends.
There they found a watery grave,
Beneath the cold and silent wave,
To be covered over by the drifting sand.

There are broken hearts and homes,
There are sorrows, there are groans,
Where was trouble, now is anguish and despair.
Where was once all smiles and light,
Now is darkness, now is night.
Where was once happy city, wreck appeared.

Tongue nor pen can never describe,
The hope, the anguish and despair,
Of the poor survivors of that awful flood,
They can never forget the day
Shawneetown was washed away,
Till they're laid beneath the cold and silent sod.

Let us rally by the scores,
To the valleys, hills, and plains,
Give our sympathy and money to their aid,
For calamity might fall,
On our loved ones, homes, and all
To be separated never to meet again.

80

THE DEATH OF CHARLIE BURGER[3]

During the prohibition era, two bootlegging gangs,
the Shelton Gang and the Burger Gang, fought for
supremacy in Southern Illinois. Burger finally drove the
Sheltons to East St. Louis and from his stronghold at
Shady Rest controlled the liquor traffic in several

counties. He maintained his position for several years by bribery of officials and murder. Brought to trial at last in Franklin County for the murder of the mayor of West City, he was convicted and hanged.

I'll tell you of a bandit,
Out in a Western state,
Who never learned his lesson
Until it was too late.
This man was bold and careless,
The leader of his gang,
But boldness did not save him
When the law said, "You must hang."

This bandit's name was Burger;
He lived at Shady Rest,
And people learned to fear him
Throughout the Middle West.
'Twas out in old West City
Joe Adams was shot down,
And then the cry of justice,
"These murders must be found."

Then Thompson was captured
And turned state's evidence.
Burger was found guilty,
For he had no defense.
He asked for a rehearing,
But this he was denied
In the county jail house
To take his life he tried.

On the 19th day of April in 1928
Away out west in Benton
Charles Burger met his fate.
Another life was ended;
Another chapter done;
Another man who gambled
In the game that can't be won.

The Ten Commandments show us
The straight and narrow way,
And if we do not heed them
Sometime we'll have to pay.
We all must face the Master,
Our final trial to stand,
And there we'll learn the meaning
Of houses built on sand.

81

THE OLD GIRL OF CAIRO TOWN[4]

An old river town with a large Negro population, Cairo was for many years a gay and wicked city of Egypt.

There was an old girl who lived in Cairo town,
And I wish to the Lord that she was dead.
She puts so many notions into my girl's head
That we can't get along, we can't get along,
We can't never get along no more.

Refrain:

Great God ain't that hard?
Me to love a girl who don't love me.

Come all the way from Cairo town,
And I never had but one dime to spend.
All the money I ever had
I done spent it on that little girl of mine,
Spent it on that little girl of mine,
Done spent it on that little girl of mine.

NOTES ON CHAPTER X

1. Through the kindness of Mr. William H. Creed, copied from the manuscript book of Mrs. Clara Walpert, Belleville.

2. Secured from Miss Millie Barnard, Shawneetown.

3. Obtained from Miss Alice Story, Harrisburg.

4. Secured from Miss Hazel Towery, Olney, who learned it from her father, Mr. B. F. Towery, Marion.

INDEX

FOLK-TALES

BALLADS AND SONGS

Shawnee Classics: A Series of Classic Regional Reprints for the Midwest